ROUTLEDGE LIBRARY EDITIONS: EMPLOYEE OWNERSHIP AND ECONOMIC DEMOCRACY

Volume 5

EMPLOYEE INVESTMENT FUNDS

EMPLOYEE INVESTMENT FUNDS

An Approach to Collective Capital Formation

RUDOLF MEIDNER
with the assistance of
ANNA HEDBORG AND
GUNNAR FOND

Routledge
Taylor & Francis Group

LONDON AND NEW YORK

First published in 1978 by George Allen & Unwin Ltd

This edition first published in 2018
by Routledge
2 Park Square, Milton Park, Abingdon, Oxon OX14 4RN

and by Routledge
711 Third Avenue, New York, NY 10017

Routledge is an imprint of the Taylor & Francis Group, an informa business

British Library Cataloguing in Publication Data
A catalogue record for this book is available from the British Library

ISBN: 978-1-138-29962-7 (Set)
ISBN: 978-1-315-12163-5 (Set) (ebk)
ISBN: 978-1-138-50660-2 (Volume 5) (hbk)
ISBN: 978-1-138-50664-0 (Volume 5) (pbk)
ISBN: 978-1-315-14698-0 (Volume 5) (ebk)

Publisher's Note
The publisher has gone to great lengths to ensure the quality of this reprint but points out that some imperfections in the original copies may be apparent.

Disclaimer
The publisher has made every effort to trace copyright holders and would welcome correspondence from those they have been unable to trace.

Employee Investment Funds

An Approach to
Collective Capital Formation

by
RUDOLF MEIDNER
with the assistance of
ANNA HEDBORG and GUNNAR FOND

London
GEORGE ALLEN & UNWIN
Boston   Sydney

First published in 1978

© This translation George Allen & Unwin (Publishers) Ltd, 1978

First published as
Kollektiv Kapitalbildning Genom Löntagarfonder
© Prisma/LO Stockholm, 1976

ISBN 0 04 331072 9

Printed in Great Britain
in 12 on 13 point Fournier
at the Alden Press, Oxford

Preface

The present study has grown out of the deliberations on wage policy at the 1971 Congress of LO, the Swedish Confederation of Trade Unions. For many years now LO has pursued a policy of solidarity in wage policy. This can be defined as a policy which seeks to relate pay to the nature of the work which an employee carries out and not to the capacity or ability-to-pay of his employer. At the 1971 Congress considerable concern was expressed about one of the consequences of this solidarity, that 'excess profits' could and did arise in more efficient companies as a result of the unions concentrating their bargaining priorities on low-pay groups. What attitude should the unions adopt to this state of affairs?

Wider issues were identified as well. Should the unions be more actively involved in capital formation in industry? Should they have a greater say in what happens to any additional company earnings? What attitude should be taken to the distribution of ownership of assets in profitable companies? As a result of this probing and questioning, the Executive of LO was asked to commission a study of worker influence, particularly via some form of collective capital formation.

Dr Rudolf Meidner, a senior economist employed by LO, was invited to head a working party within LO to study the problems in depth. At previous LO Congresses in 1961 and 1966 Meidner had put forward various suggestions which involved the establishment of branch or sector funds. So the scene had already been set. In August 1975 Meidner and

7

his colleagues produced a first version of a report on employee funds, and this was made the subject of an intensive study campaign among union members throughout the winter of 1975–6. This *consultative process* also found a focus in the responses which 18,000 union members produced to a series of written questions which Meidner and his colleagues posed in the study material. As Chapter 6 of this study in particular brings out, these replies were influential in shaping the final version of the report, which was published in time to be discussed at the LO quinquennial Congress in June 1976.

The Congress accepted the report as a basis for further work on the subject. The Executive stressed that the Meidner Report was setting out the basic principles, plus an outline sketch of possible arrangements, and the Congress agreed to keep an open mind on the details of the scheme that might finally be adopted, such as the rate of build-up of employee investment funds, the scope of the system and the administrative arrangements. Dr Meidner himself indicated that he saw his study as a contribution to the long-term solution of the problem of ownership and the distribution of power in industry and in society.

This study has proved extremely controversial in Sweden, and it has evoked a wide range of responses in various ways. A number of critical suggestions have been made and alternative proposals put forward, for example by a working group set up jointly by the Federation of Swedish Industries and the Swedish Employers' Confederation. The Central Organisation of Salaried Employees (TCO) has also published a first study of capital sharing. In that sense the Meidner Report is in the best tradition of Swedish policy making, that of making progress on important social and economic issues through intensive debate and dialogue. Before the Meidner Report had been completed a Royal Commission was appointed to examine the subject of employee influence and capital growth, and the Meidner and other studies will be grist to its mill. It is generally agreed that employee participation in the ownership of capital is an emerging theme for the 1980s, at any rate in Sweden.

This English version of the Meidner study contains the body of the original text in substantially unabridged form. The original study in Swedish contained nine appendices running to 184 pages which documented the detailed studies which provided much of the raw material for the final text. These have not been reproduced here, with the exception of a summary (in Appendix I) of the questions which were put to the participants in the consultative process and a brief indication of their responses. There are numerous references in the main text to these questions, and it may be useful to have them available in outline. The main points of some of the other appendices have been incorporated in the main text. The report also contains references to some major changes which have recently been made in Swedish labour legislation, and a summary of this legislation has been incorporated as Appendix II of this English edition.

This edition has been prepared by Dr T. L. Johnston.

Contents

Chapter 1

Background, Remit and Aims

The 1971 Congress of LO had before it a report from a special committee appointed to examine the subject of wage policy, and the committee and the Congress found themselves asking what was to be done about the problem of excess profits in many successful Swedish companies. If the trade unions put the main emphasis in their collective bargaining on solidarity and pressed the claims of poorly paid groups, did not this mean that highly profitable companies escaped with lower pay bills, and therefore higher profits, than would be the case if wage policy were to operate according to the principle of ability-to-pay? There would then exist some untapped potential for pay increases.

There was and is no intention of abandoning the wage policy based on solidarity. Emphasis on helping lower-paid workers was to continue, and the co-ordination of wage bargaining rounds was seen as the best means of promoting equity. Yet there is a dilemma. Employees in successful enterprises have found that if they do exercise pay restraint there is no way in which low-paid employees in other firms gain the benefit of their self-denial. All that happens is that profits in their own firms rise, and are excessive in the sense that the potential to pay wages on the part of these companies is not exploited to the full, owing to the principle of solidarity. Thus the more successful the policy of solidarity proves to be, the greater are the undesirable side-effects in the form of these extra profits.

Two possible solutions were envisaged in the discussion of the problem in 1971. Some scheme for taxing profits might be devised, or some form of funding might provide an answer. The idea of neutralising these excess profits was the key question in the deliberations of the 1971 Wage Policy Committee. Yet it was clear that there was also a longer-term perspective very near the surface. It was certainly desirable that companies should be profitable and thus financially sound, since this would provide greater security of employment. But it was also *essential for the community and the trade unions to acquire a greater say in the allocation of profits for investment purposes.* Thus it was not only the dilemma of wage policy solidarity which was being identified, but the far greater dilemma of how profitability and an increase in private capital formation are to be combined with democratic control over the process of capital formation itself. The trade union movement should have far more insight into and more influence over the investments of individual firms.

The concentration of ownership of capital was explicitly recognised as an issue. How should it be tackled? Perhaps there might be some kind of arrangement for redistributing profits *within* particular companies, via industrywide or sector funds, or through some kind of fund which covered the whole front along which LO operates. Various proposals originating in the Metalworkers' Union focused these matters for the 1971 Congress, and the present study has taken them into account in its analysis and recommendations.

Our primary task in this report is therefore to resolve or at least reduce the conflict between trade union solidarity and the need, for purposes of distribution policy, to restrain the profits of successful enterprises. Our second objective is *to check the concentration of wealth among traditional groups of owners* which is the inevitable concomitant of industrial self-financing. This is of course merely one part of the problem of the unequal distribution of wealth in Sweden. However, we do not propose to concern ourselves with this wider question of ownership and with the taxation of individual persons through wealth, gift and inheritance taxes and capital gains tax, but to confine ourselves to the narrower question of industrial ownership. Not only is this a part of the problem where inequality is very much in evidence; it is also one of major strategic significance.

These two objectives relate to equity and matters of distribution. A third aim is to discover ways in which we can *increase employee influence* over the economic process.

We can therefore identify three aims for this study:

(1) To complement the wage policy based on the principle of solidarity.
(2) To counteract the concentration of wealth which stems from industrial self-financing.
(3) To increase the influence which employees have over the economic process.

There is an obvious common element among these three goals, in that they are all concerned with distribution policy. There is the fear that if wage solidarity is successful this will lead to an unintended shift between the incomes of capital and labour, to the detriment of the latter. Industrial expansion largely takes place via self-financing, which means that the increase in assets (a prerequisite for growth and progress) accrues to the owners of capital. Intensive changes in the economic structure accentuate the concentration of ownership and thus of power.

There is nothing new in this. Wage solidarity has been pursued in Sweden for years. Capital growth via self-financing has been going on for as long as modern capitalism has been in existence. The process of industrial concentration is an obvious consequence of constant changes in economic structure, the scope of which was demonstrated in official studies many years ago. The concentration of economic power, also a problem of distribution, is a phenomenon which has long been noticed and discussed. What is new in the situation is that these problems are more and more being experienced as central or key problems and they have been drawn into the spotlight which has long been shining on other issues, such as inflation, the structure of the economy and intensive social reform work. The discussion at the 1971 Congress and our subsequent remit indicate that a fundamental social question of distribution has again become topical, and also that trade unionists have begun to see some connection between capital formation and the amount of influence which employees have over industrial life.

The distributive aspects of continued economic growth have also been attracting increasing attention beyond trade union circles. The most recent Long-Term Economic Survey of the Swedish economy, published in 1975, discussed the outlook towards the end of the century, and suggested that social balance would require that the gains from growth were divided equally among various groups in the community. Another group of experts, working on behalf of the Industry and Society Studies Group (SNS), observed in a recent discussion of future investment that some form of employee funds will probably provide the long-term solution to the prevailing conflict between the growth of capital and the distribution of wealth.

The objectives we have set out are thus identifying something much more pervasive than a trade union concern alone. Even within that broader framework, however, it has not proved possible for us to range absolutely freely in our inquiry. We are conscious of certain conditions which set the scene for us. A number of these are already given and generally accepted, and therefore require no detailed discussion. First and foremost among them there is the demand for full employment, or jobs for everyone. The achievement of this most fundamental of all our aims must not be prejudiced by any reforms in policies towards redistribution.

Closely related to this is the demand for *a high level of*

capital formation; indeed, this is an essential condition for high and rising employment. The Swedish economy is very exposed to foreign competition, and a high investment ratio must accordingly be sustained in order to defend our position in foreign markets. Probably few trade movements are as positive as the Swedish one in their attitude to a high level of investment, to the steady expansion and technological regeneration of the apparatus of production. This can be attributed not solely to a ready appreciation of economic relationships but primarily to a successful employment and labour market policy. Our terms of reference do not expressly require that the outcome of our mission should be the recommendation of a higher level of capital formation. Nevertheless, the assumption is a fairly obvious one; our solutions must not exacerbate the problems of providing the investment which the authorities consider desirable.

Another important stipulation is that any attempts to meet our three main objectives should be *neutral with respect to costs, wages and prices*. A measure of distributive policy which imposed a cost burden on enterprises could conceivably be shifted on to prices and be inflationary without at the same time achieving any real redistributive effect. It also follows that wage policy must not be prejudiced, and wage bargaining must be assumed to exploit to the full the possibilities for consumption, without being responsible for the relationship between consumption and saving.

Finding an arrangement which reinforces solidarity in wage policy must finally satisfy the obvious condition that it does not run counter to the main aim of that policy, which is to *equalise incomes* between different groups of employees. This means that any profit-sharing scheme which gave rise to new disparities in income within the total aggregate of employees would not be acceptable to the trade union movement.

We have accordingly to conduct our search for solutions to the problems which we have posed within a fairly narrow framework of specific objectives and conditions, and this in fact means that the range of choice among various models for redistribution is a rather limited one.

Chapter 2
Other Suggested Solutions

As was mentioned in the previous chapter, two specific proposals were suggested to the LO Congress in 1971 as methods of reinforcing wage solidarity and at the same time 'correcting' the undesirable distributional side-effects of the pay policy. The first envisaged the establishment of branch funds which would be administered by the unions; the second, higher corporation tax. Both methods deprive enterprises and their owners of some part of their profits, the former for the benefit of a number of collective employee funds, the latter for the community as a whole through the increase in tax revenue. They also have in common the point that neither involves any additional employee influence *within* a business enterprise. Obviously, then, the two methods do not entirely meet the objectives which were postulated in the preceding chapter; but they may conceivably offer some kind of partial solution, so it is worth looking at them in somewhat greater detail. We consider them in turn.

BRANCH FUNDS

Both the wage policy report to, and various proposals made at, the 1971 LO Congress suggested that branch funds could serve as 'an instrument of wages policy'. The idea has its historical roots in the traditional desire on the part of the unions to redistribute the total wage share between high- and low-wage earning groups. One suggestion made in 1938 spoke of transferring capacity-to-pay from one sector of the economy to another. Another idea floated at the 1951 Congress was for 'an equalisation fund for industries and the trade union movement'. Enterprises with high profits ought to set aside in this fund part of the pay increase from which their members abstained, and this sum would then be used to improve pay in less profitable firms. The Congress of that year torpedoed the idea as being unrealistic.

Ten years later the 1961 Congress had before it a new solution – *branch rationalisation funds* – for essentially the same problem.[1] The suggestion was viewed as one way of avoiding the consequences for the distribution of wealth which followed from the wage solidarity policy. At the same time it was thought that these funds could help to achieve other objectives, such as promoting capital formation without increasing private asset holding, and facilitating policies for actively changing the structure of industry. Resources would be channelled into these branch funds after normal bargaining between the negotiating parties on the labour market, and the funds would be utilised for such things as research, market research and training, but also, on a longer view, for direct measures of industrial policy.

If the 1951 equalisation fund idea was entirely an expression of distributive thinking, the 1961 branch fund concept was likewise coloured by the kind of thinking which was typical of the 1950s, that the trade unions should give support to the forces of expansion and growth, structural rationalisation and increased capital formation. When the 1961 Congress discussed the branch rationalisation funds the concept experienced the same fate as the earlier equalisation fund idea; the subject was quietly dropped. There was not even a need for a formal vote, since the LO Executive had not incorporated the ideas in its declaration on industrial policy.

Yet the subject was by no means dead and buried. It was

[1] See T. L. Johnston, *Economic Expansion and Structural Change*, London, 1963, esp. ch. XIII, for an exposition in English translation of these ideas.

raised again in a new expert report put to the 1966 Congress.[1]
The branch rationalisation funds had now become branch
funds; but broadly speaking the objectives were the same,
although it is worth noting that some additional aims had been
specified, such as retraining, severance pay and assisted early
retirement for workers whose jobs had been lost as a result of
rationalisation. All of these additional aims were, it will be
noted, designed to mitigate the harmful effects on the labour
force of rapid changes in industrial structure. The optimistic
note struck in the 1950s had begun to be replaced by a more
cautious outlook towards industrial change, reflecting the
sometimes bitter experiences of industrial dislocation. The
change in attitude found expression in the proposals for these
new uses for the funds; but the underlying idea remained
the same. The funds should supplement the pay policy of
solidarity.

A distinction was drawn between such funds and profit-
sharing schemes and investment wages. The funds were to be a
form of collective capital formation, 'foundations without
owners'.

Yet the proposals again evoked little interest; they
occasioned neither debate nor decision at the 1966 Congress.
Again, however, the ideas have proved robust enough to be
kept alive, and they were taken up in the wage policy report
put before the 1971 Congress.

The final paradox in all this is that in the present report we
reject the idea of branch funds in favour of other solutions,
just when we have been asked to put the branch fund idea into
some concrete shape. Experts can of course change their views,
and doubtless that it not always a bad thing. But the real
reason for the change in our thinking stems from the fresh and
much more ambitious objectives which the trade unions have
marked out.

We can still say that the allocation of resources to branch

[1] See S. D. Anderman, *Trade Unions and Technological Change*, London, 1967, for
the English version of this study.

funds, mainly from high profit firms, could lend some measure of support to wage policy. However, it is not in the interests of the unions to transfer these excess profits to inefficient enterprises. That would simply give them what was tantamount to a subsidy on wages. Such problems of weak enterprises should be tackled via labour market policy, which is the job of the whole community. If the need to support employment has been clearly established, this support should be provided through some form of social action and not via the medium of wage policy.

This is not to say that the authors of the 1961 and 1966 studies had such a 'wage clearing' arrangement in mind when they put up the suggestion for branch funds. They were thinking of the other uses of the funds which have been mentioned: training, severance pay, and so on. If the funds were to be used for such purposes, however, this would stand in the way of the *collective* capital formation which the Metalworkers' Union, for instance, had put forward as one of the objectives in its submissions to the 1971 LO Congress. A certain amount of capital would be drained away from profitable enterprises through the funds and the payments disbursed from them, without this being offset by an equivalent amount of capital formation on the part of the branch funds. This would then frustrate both a continued high level of capital formation and neutrality with respect to costs and prices. Last but not least, the collection of profits from efficient enterprises into branch funds would in no sense enhance employee influence in these firms. The growth of assets within them which was being generated by self-financing would continue to accrue to the traditional owners.

Thus we conclude that the branch fund idea, which had been a perfectly adequate means of satisfying the earlier aim of supplementing wage policy, and which also fitted well into the ongoing debate in the 1950s and 1960s about industrial policy, does not provide an adequate answer to the questions which we were asked to examine.

HIGHER CORPORATION TAX

The vast majority of the LO members who took part in the study campaign on employee funds clearly thought, in the autumn of 1975, a time of marked recession, that the question of 'excess profits' was indeed a problem. Barely 3 per cent thought that there was no problem to be tackled while 40 per cent thought that the problem would become a minor one if employee funds were once introduced. The majority, however, or 58 per cent of all those who responded to the question about excess profits, considered that, whatever the circumstances, excess profits should be tapped, for example through a higher corporation tax. This attitude fits well with the 1971 wage policy study, which spoke of the possibility of reducing excess profits via taxation. A progressive corporation tax was in fact suggested at the 1971 Congress. One proposal envisaged that, as with the investment funds scheme,[1] profits would be salted away, but employees would have a say in the uses to which they were put.

It is necessary at this point to distinguish between excess profits in the wage policy context, that of untapped potential or scope for pay increases, and excess profits as a more temporary or cyclical phenomenon. There is the final obvious point as well, which is quite independent of the two aspects just mentioned, namely, the precise construction of the corporate tax. There has undoubtedly been some confusion in the debate as to the types of profit and excess profits which were at issue, and the replies given to the questions posed in the LO study campaign must therefore be interpreted with caution. It is obvious, nevertheless, that a substantial propor-

---

[1] For recent descriptions of this scheme see *Sweden*, OECD Economic Surveys, 1975 and 1976, and H. G. Jones, *Planning and Productivity in Sweden*, London, 1976, esp. pp. 22 *et seq.*

The long-established investment fund arrangement allows companies to set aside a proportion of pre-tax profits in any year in an investment fund which can only be disbursed on projects and at a time approved by the authorities. In 1974 two additional funds, mentioned in the text, were established to deal with the buoyant profits of that period in an anti-cyclical way.

tion of those who were asked did regard collective employee funds as an appropriate means for mitigating the effects of the wage solidarity policy on profits.

Let us begin by examining briefly the question of exceptionally high profits, often limited to particular sectors of the economy and originating in abnormal export opportunities. These profits are important to wage policy, not because they are one of its consequences but because they make it more difficult to implement such a policy. This particular problem can conceivably be resolved in a number of ways, via a special prosperity tax, export levies, or the earmarking of profits, such as was applied in 1974 in the earmarked fund for improving the environment at the place of work and the special investment fund (excess profits fund). Although employees see the profits of a boom as 'excess profits', it is necessary to assess the profit position over the whole cycle. In an economy which is exposed to foreign competition and in which the trade unions are strong enough to acquire through bargaining the available potential for pay increases, profits which deserve the title or description of 'excess' occur only infrequently, as for example around the year 1951 during the Korean boom and in the extremely favourable export markets of 1974 and 1975. There were experiments in the 1950s with both special excess profits taxes and export levies which were set aside in special equalisation funds. The technical aspects of this type of arrangement are not particularly complicated, although international trade agreements do to some extent inhibit the use of export levies. Sweden is not sufficiently dominant in the world market for any products for her customers to fear that such levies would be shifted on to them in the form of higher prices for their imports. There would probably be greater understanding abroad for any Swedish action via export levies than for import restrictions. Wage pressures would be reduced if it were possible to impose export levies when particular sectors of the Swedish economy were enjoying exceptionally high profits.

In 1974–5 the Swedish government adopted another

method of 'catching excess profits'. Firms were required to set aside 20 per cent of their pre-tax profits to improve conditions at the place of work by means of accident prevention measures, improved sanitary arrangements and measures against occupational diseases. A special excess profits fund was also established, into which firms had to pay 15 per cent of their pre-tax profits for subsequent investment in plant and equipment.

The government's budget proposals for 1976 contained the information that 3,750 million crowns had been set aside in these funds, of which 1,250 million crowns had been used in 1975 and a further Sw. cr. 1,825 was likely to be drawn upon in the course of 1976.

These are substantial sums, but they cannot be regarded as constituting a slashing attack on profits; they are more in the nature of a subsidy, equivalent to a reduction in corporation tax. On the assumption that the funds have been deployed fairly rapidly for investment purposes, an assumption that seems to be a reasonable one for a substantial proportion of them, the exemption of these appropriations from taxation brings about an increase in the capital assets of their owners. The main object of the measures was to stimulate a continued high level of investment. From a distributive point of view we therefore have a preference for export profits taxes and export levies over such investment fund arrangements as methods of reducing profits in export boom conditions.

A heavier corporate tax as a permanent feature of the Swedish tax system is a much more complicated question. In terms of government revenue the existing corporation tax is of minor importance, contributing for example only 4 per cent of total central and local government tax revenues in the boom year 1974. Its redistributive effects have altered in character in the course of the years. It was originally intended to redistribute net profits from business enterprises to the whole community and thence to other groups in society via government spending programmes, but increasingly it has become a mechanism for redistributing the burden of taxation in favour of the most expansive and successful enterprises at the expense of less profitable companies. It has become increasingly plain that there is a dilemma between the government's desire to use tax policy to stimulate business investment and the undesirable distributive effects which this has had in the form of increased wealth among the owners of capital. The dilemma has been accentuated in addition by the fact that business firms are given more and more direct assistance in a variety of forms, often on industrial and employment policy grounds.

It is tempting to go on from this to recommend higher rates of corporation tax, for example by making the tax progressive, an idea which was indeed suggested at the 1971 LO Congress but rejected on the advice of the Executive. It was felt that progressive taxation was justified with regard to the taxation of property, inheritances and gifts, but it was feared that progressive taxation of business profits would have a directly damaging effect. The distributive dilemma of Swedish company taxation, with its generous incentives for growth, cannot be resolved by tightening the tax screw most severely on those companies which are expanding, thereby hampering the financing of their investment programmes.

There are of course some persuasive arguments in favour of modifying the extreme emphasis which Swedish company taxation places on profitability, growth and industrial change. It may be that Swedish industry is approaching the limits of growth and concentration. Even if the policy were to be changed, however, so that it did not provide the same selective support as in the past to successful enterprises, the fundamental problem which is the source of our remit would still remain, namely, that in every expanding economy the owners of capital require high enough profits to be able to finance new investment.

Given the type of economy which Sweden has at present, where industry is overwhelmingly privately owned and investment decisions are made by private individuals interested chiefly in profitability as the test of success, the government is in a cleft stick in designing its company tax policy. The total package of taxes, levies and contributions must be devised in such a way that it does provide the desired amount of investment, not only in aggregate but also, given the ambition with which Swedish tax policy aspires to a high degree of selectiveness, within those sectors of the economy which are to be given preferential treatment. It is then illusory to imagine that a higher rate of corporation tax can achieve major gains in the distribution of wealth and income without coming into conflict with fundamental objectives of economic policy.

The solution which we recommend does not therefore involve a severe and all-embracing increase in corporation tax. What it does mean is that a tax policy which has encouraged investment and the consolidation of assets will in future not have the adverse distributive effects which it has undoubtedly had in the past. If we are to retain the ground rules of the present system of company taxation this does, however, presuppose that the system has built into it an arrangement which enables employees to share in that growth of assets which is at once a prerequisite for and a consequence of the self-financing process which is at work within business enterprises.

In the first section of this chapter we rejected the idea of branch funds as an appropriate method for providing employees with a share in the growth of assets flowing from self-financing. Even after such funds had been established the growth of these assets would continue, though on a lower plane. For similar reasons we reject a tougher corporation tax as the principal remedy. Some increase in the rate of corporation tax is always possible, but it can never be increased to such an extent that self-financing and the accompanying growth of wealth in the hands of asset owners become impossible.

We have to accept that both profits and self-financing are

necessary features of a growth economy. The solution which we propose means that employees will obtain a share in this assets growth via the gradual allocation of profits to a system of funds which are owned and administered by the employees themselves. Our solution will also enable employees to achieve greater influence within industry, an objective which neither branch funds nor higher corporation tax can satisfy. And this objective of employee influence, it will be recalled, was one which the 1971 LO Congress regarded as extremely important.

Chapter 3

Wage Policy and the Concentration of Wealth – the Evidence

We have already remarked that the wage policy of solidarity and the concentration of wealth are two of the strategic factors in our investigation. So far we have taken the two phenomena for granted. We have assumed that the wage policy that has been adopted and pursued has been one of solidarity, and that this has favoured the owners of high-wage companies, with the result that the structure of ownership of property has become skewed. We now propose to document the correctness of these propositions.

WAGE SOLIDARITY IN ACTION

Common to all the declarations in LO specialist reports, proposals submitted to the Congress and contributions to the debate which have asked that some method should be devised for supplementing the policy of solidarity in pay, has been the assumption that the policy can produce a situation in which some proportion of the potential for pay increases is not tapped but accrues instead to owners of capital. A first approach to testing this proposition is to analyse wage trends and investigate whether the intended compression of wage differentials really has occurred. If it has not then the problem becomes irrelevant.

The evidence is quite clear as to the success of the policy of solidarity since the mid-1960s. The objective was to reduce the wage differentials between various LO groups, while awaiting a more comprehensive and sophisticated system based on job evaluation. The results can be measured by reference to the change in the dispersion of wages around the average in manufacturing industry. Partly as a consequence of the emphasis which LO over a period of years has placed on a low-wage drive, this dispersion has been reduced and differentials have narrowed. It is not certain that this compression is precisely the one which we should have wished to achieve if a comprehensive system of job evaluation had been available. But that is not relevant to our argument. The essential point is that wage policy has been conducted in a co-ordinated form, that the object is to achieve greater equity in pay as between groups and individuals, and that in recent years these efforts have manifestly produced results.[1]

This statement can be supported in a number of ways, all of them deficient in some respect. One rather crude but very illuminating method is to examine how the relative positions of the various collective agreements in the bargaining sector occupied by LO and SAF (the Swedish Employers' Confederation) have altered since about 1960. Figure 1 shows the trend in earnings according to this method. The upper curve represents the average for those agreements which lay above the industrial average, and the lower curve that for the agreements below the average. Measured in this way, the spread of wages has declined by almost a half in fifteen years.

Sceptics challenge the testimony of these figures by advancing the hypothesis that the policy of solidarity in pay has not made any major contribution to this process of equalisation; it would have happened anyway, by virtue of market forces and without such a policy. Unfortunately for the sceptics, the long-

---

[1] Most of the statistical material used in this section is taken from an article by Ingvar Ohlsson, on the results and problems of the wage policy of solidarity, which was published in *Tiden* in 1975.

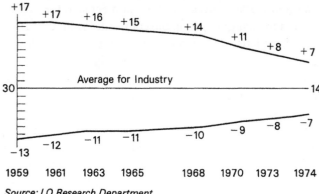

Source: LO Research Department

Figure 1   *Growth of earnings – deviation from industrial average 1959–74*

drawn-out wage negotiations in 1969 and 1971 provided a unique opportunity to study wage movements during two periods when no new agreements had been concluded and the play of market forces was thus free to operate on wage determination without any interference from the low-wage strategy. The results are striking. In both periods, 1968–9 and 1970–1, there was a break in the trend, and the gap between high- and low-wage agreements *widened*. It is hard to imagine a more convincing proof of the thesis that solidarity has achieved its successes in the teeth of market forces.

The method which has been used to measure the spread of wages is a fairly crude one, in that it measures the spread *between*, but not *within*, collective agreements. Since 1970, statistics have been available on an individual basis for 75 to 80 per cent of the workers in the LO-SAF sector, and this makes possible a very much better analysis of wage trends. It appears that the compression of differentials has proceeded somewhat more rapidly *between* than *within* collective agreements.

The policy of wage solidarity simply has to produce results –

and they have been surprisingly good results, given the strength of market forces – if the union demand for a clawback of profits from highly profitable companies is to have any kind of firm foundation. But while this is a necessary condition it is not sufficient on its own. Obviously, high profits can occur, and mostly do, in other ways than via the unexploited potential for pay increases (sometimes called 'excess profits') and, conversely, many low-profit companies have high-wage groups. A thoroughgoing analysis of the relationship between profitability and pay would be needed to establish whether and to what extent restraint on the part of highly paid groups does lead to increases in profits. The influence on the wage situation of a number of factors, such as the composition of the labour force with respect to jobs and qualifications, systems of payment, geographical location of the plant and the structure of the local labour market, would all have to be examined. This is a sophisticated research undertaking, on which no one has yet embarked.

One study which was carried out for the purpose of this report analysed information about the relationship between profitability and pay in some eighty engineering firms in the period 1970–3.[1] The analysis shows that the relationship is a weak one. Broadly speaking, there are as many high-wage companies among the profitable as the less profitable companies. Conversely, it is by no means unusual for engineering firms which are not particularly profitable, relatively speaking, to have relatively high wages. For the time being, therefore, caution must be exercised in speaking generally about 'excess profits' as a consequence of the wage solidarity policy.

Even greater caution is in order when we assess the influence which the wage policy has had on trends in the wage share in the economy. The available statistics are admittedly imperfect, but they provide no support for the assumption that the success

[1] Appendix IV of the original Swedish version of the study contains the detail of this investigation.

of pay solidarity should have led wage earners as a whole to lose out to capital. One tentative hypothesis is that the wage policy of solidarity does not affect the *level* of profits, or the relationship between profits and pay in the aggregate, but that it does affect the *structure* of profits. It would accordingly favour the high-wage companies at the expense of the remainder. To the extent that high-wage companies are identical with high-profit companies, the wage policy reinforces the effect which our growth-promoting corporation tax is endeavouring to achieve.

The relationship between wage policy and the structure of profits is thus complicated and far from clear-cut. Nevertheless, strong arguments can be adduced for reinforcing the pay policy of solidarity with a mechanism for skimming off profits, via tax or in some other way, from firms which are profitable. In principle, pay restraint does give rise to profit increases in certain sectors of industry which would not otherwise have occurred. Similarly, the low-pay drive results in reduced profits in other enterprises, which are not necessarily low-profit firms. As we have already suggested, the total effect of pay solidarity on the trend of profits cannot be elucidated without an analysis in depth.

From a trade union point of view the effect of the wage policy on the profitability of particular firms or sectors is not unimportant, however, irrespective of whether 'excess profits' and reductions in profits cancel out or not. Restraint *vis-à-vis* highly profitable companies frequently poses a severe test for the highly paid groups; it creates strains and stresses and threatens to undermine union solidarity. These tensions can be assuaged via wage drift, in the sense that (as was shown above) market forces in part modify the objectives of wage policy. But high-wage drift distorts the low-wage profile which LO is pursuing, and other groups, particularly those with rigid systems of payment, then demand compensation. In other words, co-ordination of wage policy comes under serious pressure, whether the highly paid groups are capable of following the Commandment of Co-ordination or market forces work against these endeavours.

If the trade union movement wishes to continue to defend the wage policy of solidarity – and that is the obvious datum for our whole argument – it ought to be supported by some method for skimming off profits from those companies which are favoured by the policy.

THE DISTRIBUTION OF OWNERSHIP

The now familiar proposition that the wage policy of solidarity has favoured owners of capital at the expense of the totality of employees could conceivably be incorrect; yet the structure of wealth can still alter in a manner which is undesirable from the point of view of equality. This relates to the point made at the 1971 LO Congress, that industrial self-financing leads to the continued concentration of wealth in the hands of traditional property-owning groups. It is clear from the debate on this topic in a number of Western European countries that it is the very fact that this growth in capital does *and must* occur *within* business enterprises which provides the starting-point for various schemes of profit sharing via the setting-up of funds. In stressing that they wanted to make more resources available for investment without this producing adverse effects on the distribution of wealth, the Swedish trade union advocates were touching on one of the crucial problems in the process of capital formation, and one that cannot be resolved with the aid either of wage or tax policies.

We are thus interested solely in one part of capital accumulation and the total mass of property. In principle, the cry for justice can relate to the *whole* structure of property, which does of course reflect major inequities. In Sweden 40 per cent of those who are liable to submit tax returns own no net assets at all, and the net assets of a further 55 per cent are below the tax liability threshold. Something of the order of half of total personal assets in Sweden are owned by 5 per cent of those who are required to submit tax returns. This may be inequitable, and major reforms may be needed; but our focus of attention is none the less ownership in industry, as those who raised the subject in 1971 intended.

The statistics available on this topic are poor and out-of-date, but some features are nevertheless very clear. The value of industrial capital constitutes only one-sixth of total real capital in Sweden, and four-fifths of industry's capital is owned by companies. It is the owners of this share capital, in itself a small proportion of her national assets, who largely determine the allocation of the productive resources of the country. Share capital can in this sense be described as 'strategic' capital, as distinct from other categories of capital such as durable consumer goods and real estate. In its various uses this strategic capital affects every aspect of the life of the community, such as employment, incomes, regional dispersion and foreign trade. The question of share ownership and its distribution is consequently much more than one of social justice; it is a matter of ensuring that employees do have a greater say in shaping economic and industrial policy.

An inquiry which was carried out in late 1975 showed that just over 700,000 persons in Sweden own shares, an increase of several hundred thousand over the position some ten years ago. The growth of unit trusts is an expression of the fact that share ownership as a form of saving is on the increase in Sweden; indeed, this is natural, since this form of saving usually does become more important in countries in which living standards are rising. It is also regarded as beneficial to the national economy, since a broadening of saving through share ownership injects more risk capital into industry. In general, share ownership as a form of saving provides better protection against inflation than saving through the medium of the banks.

However, these comparatively large figures for the number of shareholders and the broadening of share ownership ought not to conceal the point that share ownership is very unevenly distributed. The vast majority have very small holdings while a few persons and institutions have very large holdings. Information about the distribution of share ownership has previously become available only in connection with the work of the official Committee on Concentration, and this related to the mid-1960s. In a sample of fifteen quoted companies, on average 0·2 per cent of the shareholders owned 25 per cent of the capital, 2 per cent owned 50 per cent, and 10 per cent owned no less than 75 per cent. Many people have argued that the distribution of share ownership has become much more even since then, but this conjecture is hardly supported by a study which we made of 63 of the total of some 140 quoted companies.[1] Indeed, the opposite is the case.

So far we have included in the term shareholders both individual and legal persons. The continuing concentration of share ownership is in part an expression of a shift in the stock market away from private to institutional holders. In 1950 individual persons owned 75 per cent of shares, whereas the figure was only 55 to 60 per cent in 1970.[2] Our statistical material shows the figure falling to barely 53 per cent. Investment companies, which are of course largely owned in turn by private persons, accounted for $13\frac{1}{2}$ per cent, family trusts, pension funds and insurance companies for 15 per cent. In 1975, unit trusts, whose shareholders can without exception be described as small savers, held less than 1 per cent of all the shares in the sixty-three companies which we studied.

The structure of ownership among private persons (owning 53 per cent of all shares) is particularly interesting. As expected,

[1] Appendix I of the original study contains detail on the distribution of share ownership. On average, 0·15 per cent of shareholders in 1975 owned 32 per cent of the shares (with more than 20,000 shares each), 0·45 per cent owned 47 per cent and 3 per cent owned 66 per cent. Share ownership has thus become more concentrated. The 'small savers' with fewer than 500 shares held $97\frac{1}{2}$ per cent of all blocks of shares in 1975, but they owned a mere 35 per cent of all the shares. Even companies with a very large number of shareholders have this skewed distribution; for example, in Volvo over 100,000 small shareholders own 50 per cent of the shares, while the nine largest own 15 per cent.

[2] Roland Spånt, *Förmögenhetsfordelningen i Sverige* (The Distribution of Wealth in Sweden), Falköping, 1975.

the structure is less uneven when institutional holders are excluded. Of all private persons who own shares in the sixty-three companies, 98½ per cent own 66 per cent of the shares held by individual persons. To put the point the other way, 1½ per cent of all private shareholders own as much as 34 per cent of all the shares which are privately held. This imbalance emerges clearly if one looks at the really large shareholders with blocks of more than 2,000 shares. They hold only 0·2 per cent of the blocks of shares owned by individual persons, but they own not less than 18 per cent of that part of the issued share capital held by private persons.

HOW DO SHAREHOLDERS EXERCISE THEIR VOTING RIGHTS?

With some few exceptions nowadays, share ownership entitles the holder to exercise the right to vote at company annual meetings. The main duty of the annual meeting of shareholders is to approve the management of a company by the board in the year ended, to determine dividends, and elect the board. Company annual meetings are usually rather undramatic and sparsely attended gatherings, and it is easy to form the impression that real power lies with the management, which frequently has only a small shareholding interest in many of our quoted companies. Cases do occur where there is a combination of strong and expert management and a diffuse ownership which is primarily interested in income or capital growth from the shares held, but in critical situations it may be of the utmost importance for the owners to exercise real control. For major decisions affecting the future of a company with regard to mergers, acquisitions and sales of companies in whole or part, closures, relocation, removal to another country, and so forth, it may be essential to have a firm grip on the supreme decision-making body, the annual meeting. Only the owners, who in the largest companies are without exception a minority of all the shareholders, can exercise this power, quite in accordance with the rules of the Companies Act. There are examples, not least from the recent feverish merger activity in Swedish trade and industry, of the owners making decisions over the heads of the management. The theory of the managerial revolution provides a seductive argument for belittling the importance of ownership in large Swedish industries, but in reality management is severely circumscribed.

Who, then, does make the decisions at annual meetings, decisions which are in the main of a largely routine character but which can sometimes be quite crucial? We have probed this question by studying the proceedings of the annual meetings of more than fifty of our quoted companies, and the following are the main points to emerge.[1]

Annual meetings are generally poorly attended, at the most by a few hundred persons who usually account for less than 1 per cent of all the shareholders. It is exceptional for more than 2 per cent to be present. But those few who do find it worth taking the trouble to attend most frequently represent a large proportion of the issued capital of the company. In half the cases we examined those present represented between 25 and 50 per cent of the total voting entitlement. In a further third, 50 to 80 per cent of the total voting entitlement was represented. In other words, it is the major shareholders, either individuals or legal persons, who exercise their voting rights at company annual meetings. Pride of place goes to the board members, who are frequently not quite so propertyless as the talk of specialist boards of directors might lead one to imagine. On average, the board owns close on 6 per cent of the votes represented at annual meetings. However, it is customary for the board members to obtain proxies from other shareholders, thereby strengthening their voting power. In the companies which we studied the board alone could achieve a majority in twenty-one out of fifty-four cases (nearly 40 per cent) in this way. It is important to bear in mind in this connection that

[1] The detailed results are given in Appendix II of the original Swedish study.

under the Companies Act the annual meeting is the body which scrutinises the board, but in fact there is a far-reaching identity between this controlling body and the group which it is supposed to be controlling.

Nor do other major shareholders outside the board neglect to obtain proxies, with the result that the annual meetings of our large companies are run by a veritable oligarchy, in full conformity with prevailing legislation and regulations. At sixteen of the fifty-four annual meetings one person had a voting majority, and in a further sixteen two persons could dictate what happened. A further fifteen annual meetings would have to be included to cover situations where three persons could decide. This is a remarkable state of affairs from the standpoint of democracy, that in close on 90 per cent of the companies we examined it required at the most three persons to reach accord (on the basis of their own holdings plus proxies) for them to control a majority of the votes at the annual meeting. In none of the fifty-four companies were more than six persons required to achieve this majority.

Compare these results with the similar investigation which the Concentration Committee undertook over ten years ago. In 1963 the voting majority in three-quarters of the quoted companies studied was divided among not more than three persons. The corresponding figure for our fifty-four companies was nine-tenths. In all probability, therefore, the concentration of voting power at company meetings has increased further in the past ten years.

To summarise, share ownership in Sweden is heavily concentrated, and this process of concentration appears to be continuing. Since the larger shareholders both make better use of their voting entitlement and also reinforce this strongly by means of proxies, the imbalance at company meetings, the supreme decision-making body, is multiplied many times over. It is the rule rather than the exception for two or three shareholders to hold a voting majority at a company annual meeting. This oligarchy has no counterpart anywhere in our democratic society. Those who see in a widening of share ownership a route towards greater influence for the small shareholder must ponder the point that this same domination by a few persons prevails in our most popular companies with many thousands of small shareholders. The spread of ownership as a way of making industry truly democratic scarcely merits even being termed a sham solution.

Chapter 4

The Design of Employee Investment Funds

Our objectives, it will be recalled, are to supplement solidarity in wages policy, to counteract the concentration of assets which flows from self-financing and to increase employee influence in industry. Any scheme designed to achieve these aims must also satisfy certain conditions. There must be no adverse effects on employment and on capital formation. Wage policy must not be stifled. The scheme must be neutral with regard to costs and prices. It must not obstruct the road to greater equality of incomes. In other words, the system should achieve our three objectives without prejudicing other important aims of economic and wages policy.

Some of those who have contributed to the debate on this agenda have suggested that it would have been more appropriate to tackle the problems via a package of measures rather than through searching for some 'comprehensive solution'. It would be technically easier, in their judgement, and it would also lead to less intervention in the existing social system than some comprehensive solution such as a system of collectively owned employee funds. The debate which raged in the autumn of 1975 brought out some of the main approaches which such commentators had in mind.

It was thought that the problem of *excess profits and pay*

41

solidarity could best be resolved via some form of clearing system for wages, by the allocation of shares to sector funds or via the taxation of profits. The *concentration of wealth and property* could be tackled via savings incentives, individual profit-sharing schemes, and tougher taxation of property, inheritances and gifts, and by capital gains taxes. *Employee influence* was surely adequately catered for through the new labour legislation. The logical conclusion from these various strands of argument was that a system of employee funds was to be regarded not only as somewhat risky but as quite superfluous to boot.

Such arguments may seem fairly plausible, but closer inspection discloses some serious weaknesses. We proceed to deal with the arguments in turn.

(a) *Solidarity and excess profits.* The idea of setting up some kind of clearing system for wages as between high- and low-profit enterprises to provide reinforcement for the solidarity pay policy does, or at any rate did, evoke a sympathetic response in trade union circles. One weakness in this line of argument which was previously somewhat overlooked was that, as we have pointed out earlier, low-profit firms are not always identical with low-wage enterprises. This proposal then runs the risk of transferring funds from firms with high wages and low profits to firms which are profitable and pay low wages. A stronger objection relates to the opposite situation, which is probably more common, namely, that profits are transferred from highly productive firms, with satisfactory capacity-to-pay, to unprofitable enterprises. An arrangement of this kind would fit rather ill with our specification of strong and competitive industries as a guarantee of rising standards of living and high employment. Similar objections can be raised against the proposals for sector funds or higher taxes on profits. In both cases the profits of highly productive enterprises would be siphoned off and capital formation might be put at risk.

(b) *The concentration of assets.* Many proposals have been put forward for countering the concentration of wealth and its accompanying power, but their efficacy can be questioned. It is a commonly held view that the structure of wealth would be decisively altered by an increase in individual saving. However, it is difficult to see how private saving by individuals could be increased without some strong tax incentives (subsidies), a method which is extremely dubious from the standpoint of policies towards distribution. It is equally difficult to see how an increase in saving on the part of individual employees would reduce the wealth of owners of capital. If the volume of saving did rise to such an extent that it had a dampening effect on the whole economy, policy measures would be called for to neutralise this by stimulating demand.

Profit-sharing schemes which incorporate the right for the individual to dispose of his shares have often been proposed as a genuine alternative to employee funds, but the trade union movement has steadfastly rejected this route as irreconcilable with solidarity in wage policy. There are fundamental economic as well as ideological objections to profit sharing as a solution. What may appear possible or even appropriate for the individual firm and its employees on the micro plane may be improper from a macro viewpoint. Firms can certainly distribute profit shares to their staff, but unless savings habits change the distribution of profit shares makes claims on the total resources which are available for consumption in the economy. If enough firms were to operate a system of profit sharing the profit shares would in effect become wage and salary shares. The wage policy founded on solidarity would be undermined, without the total body of employees being able to raise their consumption. The only way in which asset holding among employees can be increased is through the shares of profits being saved in some permanent form by the recipients. We have just expressed our doubts as to whether such saving can be achieved voluntarily. As far as we are aware, none of the advocates of profit-sharing systems has recommended that such profit shares do have to be saved via some kind of obligatory savings scheme, so there is no need to discuss the matter here, particularly since such a solution does not appear to be acceptable to the trade unions either.

To tone down the concentration of wealth by appropriate tax measures is on the other hand a realistic alternative. Higher property and capital gains taxes come to mind, and they would apply not only to shares but to other types of asset, particularly real estate, which does of course constitute by far the largest part of privately owned assets. Suggestions along these lines by LO have produced a strong reaction from the non-socialist political parties, and this should be taken as a sign that these groups in fact do not wish to see such a tax increase. The main reason why we do not propose this particular route as a means of counteracting the concentration of assets is that our remit is limited to dealing with that part of assets growth which accompanies business self-financing. The much more comprehensive question of the taxation of capital and capital gains is outside our assignment. In any case it is being examined at the present time by a number of official committees.

(c) *Employee influence.* It is correct that the recent reforms in labour legislation do involve a very major step on the road to economic democracy. However, the 1971 LO Congress took the position that employee influence based on the input of capital into enterprises need not be excluded as a possibility, and we have obviously had to follow this pointer in our investigations. The position which that Congress adopted also commands very firm support among the union membership; about 90 per cent of those who participated in the consultative process on collective employee funds reckoned that it was absolutely imperative or important for the employees to be given ownership rights in firms in order to increase their influence. We would have been guilty of serious neglect of both the Congress and of membership opinion if we had sought for solutions along other avenues.

All of these packages which we have now reviewed have one feature in common. They fail to put a stop to the growth of assets and wealth in the hands of capital owners which accompanies industrial self-financing. To adopt any of them would be to leave one of our essential tasks unresolved. By contrast, a system of collective employee funds which are accumulated by means of successive allocations of profits does not appear to be superfluous; indeed, it is an appropriate device for achieving the three objectives which we have repeatedly articulated. As distinct from other alternatives, such as individual profit-sharing schemes, investment wages or excess profits funds of the type used in 1974, a system of employee investment funds ought to be constructed in such a way that it does involve real participation in capital formation on the part of the employees or, to put it another way, a real sharing of profit as between the owners of capital and the employees.

If this end is to be achieved, it is essential that that part of the growth in assets which accrues to the employees *remains as working capital within the enterprise*. We cannot stress this enough. The main objective would be frustrated if there were to be any withdrawals from the capital of the funds on a group or individual basis. To many this fundamental requirement of a system of employee investment funds may appear strange. It has sometimes been described in the debate as the expression of an authoritarian mentality which seeks to limit the free right of disposal on the part of the private individual in favour of a bureaucratically governed group.

In reality, however, the choice is not between the individual's free right to dispose over a share of profits and collective power, but between illusory profit-sharing and real profit-sharing.

We can bring out the point most readily by looking at the activities of a consumers' co-operative. The shareholders create a joint capital by acting on a co-operative basis. A small part of the profit of the movement is repaid to the members in the form of a rebate, but the larger portion remains in the association and thus within the whole consumer co-operative enterprise complex. The capital is continually being augmented through the modernisation of retail shops, opening of new department stores, expansion of co-operatively owned industries, and so on. This very substantial total capital is owned in Sweden by 1,800,000 households. None of the individual members receives a certificate for his or her share of these assets, still less can members demand to withdraw 'their' share of the co-operative capital. Every withdrawal of that type would weaken the economy of the co-operative. If it were to be possible for many members to withdraw their share of the capital for consumption purposes or for investing in some other activity, the very existence of the co-operative would be imperilled. The fact that it is not possible to make such individual withdrawals of capital is not due to any authoritarian attitude on the part of the management. It is entirely due to the realisation on the part of the members that consumer co-operation can only expand and develop provided the accumulated capital remains within the group.

This whole line of reasoning can be applied by analogy to a scheme of employee investment funds. We can visualise the whole of our privately owned large-scale industry as one single complex (an idea, incidentally, which may not be particularly unrealistic in the long run, given present trends to concentration). The activity of the complex yields a profit, which is largely ploughed back into new investment, and part of the new capital thus created accrues to the employees as a group. Irrespective of who owns it, the total stock of capital forms the foundation of our economic and social progress. It is nothing less than a gross illusion to give the individual partner (the employee) the opportunity to dispose as he sees fit over 'his' or 'her' share. It is of doubtful value to the individual, and obviously harmful in the long run not only to the employees as a group but to the whole community.

THE CONSTRUCTION OF EMPLOYEE INVESTMENT
FUNDS

(i) *Directed issues of employee shares*

The *modus operandi* of employee investment funds can be
described quite succinctly in the following terms. The ownership of part of the profits which are ploughed into an enterprise is simply transferred from the previous owners to the
employees as a collective. A proportion – we propose 20 per
cent – of the profit is set aside for the employees. This money
does not however leave the business. Instead, a company
issues shares to that amount, and these are transmitted to the
employee fund. Legislation will be required to regulate the
forms in which these directed or restricted share issues are
made, irrespective of whether a system of funds could be set
up via collective bargaining negotiations.

Share issues, which is what we have in mind, normally
accrue to existing shareholders. A scrip or bonus issue means
that the worth of a company is divided into a larger number of
shares. Each shareholder is entitled to a number of shares such
that his allocation of the scrip issue is as large as his share of
the ownership of the enterprise prior to the bonus issue.
Thus a scrip issue does not normally alter the distribution of
ownership. Everyone owns as much as he did before, but
divided among a larger number of shares. Share issues restricted
or directed to employee funds, on the other hand, would
gradually shift the weight of ownership towards the employees,
since the fund would receive each year an issue of shares
without the remaining shareholders having a similar entitlement. If, over and above this, the annual meeting of the company were to decide on scrip issues of the normal type, the
rate at which the employee fund grew in an enterprise would
not on the other hand be altered. The employee fund would be
entitled to receive its portion of the bonus issue in proportion
to the holding which it had already acquired, leaving the structure of ownership unchanged.

Other questions would also have to be dealt with through legislation. In its existing form the Companies Act is so flexible that it would permit transactions undertaken with a view to countering the growth and influence of employee funds within a company. A review of the Act will be needed, not of course in order to provide special arrangements for employee funds as shareholders but to deal with the obvious point that these funds would represent a steadily growing owner in all large companies, a new phenomenon which the Companies Act did not contemplate. Thus the rules in the Act which are intended to protect minorities and ensure equal treatment for different owners do not automatically apply. Any special rules ought to be based on the premiss that the funds will be guaranteed a legitimate influence. We have to bear in mind the possibility that established shareholders, who have to relinquish a proportion of their profits to a fund, will combine in opposition to the fund.

A company may have various types of share, and the employee fund should receive allocations of the different types of share in the same proportion as these occur in the company's capital structure. Companies can, for example, issue shares with differing voting entitlements, and some have different series of shares with varying voting rights, such as A or B shares. Nowadays, no share can have voting rights more than ten times greater than that of any other share, although examples still exist of old B shares which have only one-thousandth part of a vote. In L. M. Ericsson some 16 per cent of the shares have nearly 190 times as many votes as the remaining 84 per cent of the shares. If no rules existed which provided for the types of shares to which an employee fund was entitled, they might be issued with shares with a lower voting entitlement than the shares of established shareholders.

The Companies Act contains one rule which means that, in the absence of anything to the contrary in the articles of association, no one may vote for more than 20 per cent of the share capital represented at an annual meeting. Most companies have abrogated this rule and permit every individual to vote for the full number of shares which he or she owns. This type of restriction on voting rights ought not to be reintroduced, in case it is used to restrict the influence of employee voting.

A *new issue* of shares enables a company to obtain new capital by issuing new shares. Normally, the new shares are offered as 'rights' to existing shareholders, so that they can retain their existing proportion of the capital of the company by subscribing for their allocation of the new issue. Obviously, then, an employee investment fund must be able to participate in any new share issues made if it is not to experience a decline in its relative position. Funds should accordingly utilise part of the dividends that accrue from their aggregate holdings for the purpose of taking up their rights. It is of course conceivable in theory that existing shareholders may seek to postpone a takeover on the part of the fund by making such large issues of new shares that the employee fund cannot finance the purchase of its allocation. But this is probably no more than a theoretical problem. It is hardly likely that so much new risk capital could be mobilised to postpone a takeover which eventually becomes inevitable. In any case an employee investment fund could offer its allocation of shares to the fourth National Pension Fund (set up in 1974 for the purpose of investing in the ordinary shares of selected companies), if the stream of new issues were to exceed its available resources.

One possibility which may be a more real one is for a company annual meeting to direct or restrict a new share issue to a particular group. Used systematically, such a power could be deployed to prevent an employee fund achieving a critical voting capacity. There are on the other hand situations in which restricted share issues may be desirable or necessary for the company from the standpoint of the employee fund as well, for example when a rapid period of growth requires a major injection of new capital which perhaps only the Pension Fund can digest. One possible method of ensuring that restricted issues were not used for the express purpose of obstructing the employee funds would be for the funds to be given a right of veto over any transactions which did involve the funds in shifts of ownership within a company.

It is not intended that a fund should deal in its holdings of shares, with the one exception of a merger situation. After a merger the fund ought of course to own the same proportion of the new enterprise as corresponds to a weighed average of its share of the previous company. It is conceivable that an existing majority of owners could try to postpone, though they could not ultimately prevent, a shift in power towards the employee fund by merging companies which had a high proportion of employee share ownership with firms in which the employee share was smaller. The Companies Act does specify rules about qualified majorities in merger situations, but the minority rules are inadequate for the employee fund; any kind of threshold could lead the previous shareholders to combine and ensure that the fund did not pass the critical threshold which entitled it to the special protection under the Act for minority groups. It is therefore more appropriate to have a general right of veto for the fund over any transactions which may alter its share of ownership.

The device of restricted employee share issues does assume that the companies which are included in our proposals are limited liability companies. There are, however, other forms of business aimed at profit making which are organised in other types of company. Partnerships and private companies occur particularly among small enterprises, though there are admittedly some very large partnerships.

It might be reasonable to require businesses of a certain size in principle to be carried on as limited liability companies. This would not only facilitate the introduction of a system of employee funds. Under existing legislation an entrepreneur chooses for himself the form in which he wishes to conduct his business, and this leads naturally to the company form being selected in the light of tax or accountability rules. Legislation in general, but perhaps tax legislation in particular, would be greatly facilitated if the legislator could assume that every type of activity was conducted in the company form intended for the type of business in question. Large business enterprises would then be limited liability companies; but this would not be permissible for small individual entrepreneurs who really do put their all into their business.

Partnerships and private companies could be used as the organisational forms for small enterprises. An investigation is currently being conducted concerning a particular form of company for small businessmen who may wish to carry on their affairs with a limited amount of personal liability, but without being forced to become limited liability companies. If a new form of company of this nature were to be established, it would then be easier as well to adapt the limited liability form of company to the particular category of large-scale business enterprises. Such businesses would then be required to be conducted in the form which had been designed for them.

(ii) *Profits as the basis of calculation*
Since the object of the funds is to transfer the right of ownership of part of the growth in a company's assets to the employees, the most appropriate basis of calculation for this purpose is profit. Only by linking appropriations to the fund to profits do we obtain a direct relationship between the growth of the fund in the individual enterprise and the expansion of the enterprise through self-financing. No less important from our standpoint is that it is only by being linked to profits that the funds can complement the solidarity wages policy. The higher the profits which result from wage restraint, the more rapidly will the fund grow if the amount of the appropriation is made to depend on profit.

Unfortunately, profit is not an altogether unambiguous concept. Profit emerges as the difference between a firm's receipts or income and its costs. In general it is possible to determine *income* with a reasonable degree of precision in monetary terms. The only really serious method of manipulating it would be by systematically charging too low prices for a company's own products, and most firms have no reason to undertake this kind of juggling. It is in their interest to charge as high prices as possible. But if it is the amount of profit that is to determine the size of the allocations to the employee investment fund, some companies may endeavour to dispose of the profits in such a way that they fall outside the system. Multinational companies with parent or subsidiary companies in other countries present the most important and complex risks in this connection. Internal or shadow pricing may be used by international companies at the expense of the Swedish companies in the group, and profits which ought properly to be assigned to Sweden may be taken out in other countries. This procedure is already illegal under current tax legislation, but it is very difficult for the fiscal authorities to monitor it.

The *cost* side poses much more difficult problems, since there are no simple or uniform rules for what are to be regarded as costs. Purchases of inputs from outside a firm are fairly straightforward; but problems arise with regard to the internal allocation of costs, as between foreign and domestic parts of an enterprise, with regard to patent and licensing costs, and selling, marketing, product development and administrative costs. In our section on multinational companies we return to the problem of international firms which report unreasonably low profits in Sweden year after year.

The major determinant of reported profits is, however, the rules which govern the costs that are incurred through the depreciation of capital. The timing of depreciation provisions can affect reported profits. Firms like to depreciate as much as possible early in the life of an asset and set this against any profits tax liability, thus retaining funds within the enterprise which would otherwise have been paid out in tax. This procedure can be likened to an interest-free loan or tax credit from the central and local governments. Expanding firms which are continually increasing investment can shift the tax liability forward in time, and during the whole period of expansion their reported profits will systematically be too low. Tax legislation therefore has to set limits to the rate at which firms may depreciate assets. Swedish tax legislation is acknowledged to be very generous in the write-off rates which it permits for investment and for stock depreciation, so generous in fact that industry as a whole had in 1975 accumulated 27,000 million crowns in tax credits, equal to about 11 per cent of the total aggregate value of inventories, equipment and buildings.

Apart from the special problems associated with international companies, there are problems at the other end of the scale with very small firms. Not only may their accounting practices be inadequate; it may also be possible for them to report little or no profit, depending on what 'profit' is withdrawn in the form of salaries or other benefits. So there are undoubtedly major difficulties in using profits as the basis of calculation for the employee investment fund system. Of course there is no need to apprehend a *worse* measure of profit than that used in fiscal law; indeed, there are grounds for holding that it should be possible to arrive at a better measure of profit.

The prospects of active control ought to be greater in the case of the funds than they are for the tax authorities. In the first place, at least the large quoted companies with many Swedish owners can scarcely stop reporting profits in Sweden. In order to raise capital they have to report profits sufficiently large to provide a reasonable dividend return to their Swedish owners. Moreover, it is undoubtedly the case that the tax and customs authorities in more and more countries are striving to increase their control over the activities of large enterprises in particular. In addition to this, or perhaps because of it, accounting practices of most large enterprises are increasingly tending to report profits where they originate. We should not underestimate the difficulties, nor the likelihood of firms adjusting their actions in the event of funds being established. But at least one can assume reasonable reporting standards in the case of large enterprises with a diffuse ownership. The position is quite different in small family-dominated firms, where dividends are in addition often of no significance. It is of course the larger companies which are of particular interest to the system of employee investment funds.

In the second place, it is reasonable to assume that the growth of the funds will be of interest to those employed in the enterprises covered by them, and that they will monitor the actions of their firms. The outlook for this kind of surveillance will also improve with the progress of the system of employee consultants, economic committees and the extended obligations on the part of companies to provide information about their activities.[1]

Surveillance of this kind will clearly require rules which prescribe what is and is not to be permitted *vis-à-vis* the funds. We cannot rely entirely on the rules of tax law here, for instance with regard to the size of the salaries which people pay themselves in partnerships or in small family businesses.

The measure of profit used to determine the appropriations to the employee funds should of course be profits *prior to* various 'appropriations out of profits', to use an accounting phrase.

Depreciation and write-off periods for capital and inventories are intimately connected with the method used to value the shares which are to be allocated to the funds each year. Let us now turn to this problem in detail.

(iii) *The valuation of employee shares*
An annual valuation of a company will be required to determine how many shares can be allocated out of the sum set aside for the employee fund. A value for each share can be determined by dividing the worth of the enterprise by the number of shares in it already in existence, and this price can then be used in issuing shares to the fund.

For quoted companies share prices are available which are determined by the stock market. There are certain attractions

[1] See Appendix II for a fuller discussion of recent labour legislation.

about using these market quotations, in the sense that the annual valuation could then take place quite automatically. But the method also has certain disadvantages. The Swedish stock exchange is an exceedingly small market, and only a very small proportion of the shares of companies quoted on it are turned over in the market in the course of a year. Thus it is quite possible for large shareholders to manipulate the market. Equally, we cannot exclude the possibility that the system of employee funds will itself affect stock market quotations. In straightforward economic terms, the very introduction of a system based on an appropriation out of profits, which means that the existing shareholders experience a lower return, should lead to a fall in share prices which reflects the decline in the future expected yield. In addition to this economic response there may, however, be a less predictable psychological reaction. If the quoted market price were to be applied for valuation purposes, every fall in price in the shares of a company would mean that the employee fund obtained more shares out of its allocation from profits. The possibility of panic selling in the face of the prospect of an imminent total assumption of power by the employee investment fund could not then be excluded.

We cannot believe that such a panic reaction would be warranted or even likely; nevertheless, it may still be worthwhile countering the possibility by applying some sort of substantive valuation based on the actual assets of the company. This would mean that the individual enterprise could predict the consequences for it of the introduction of the funds, and another advantage would be that the same system of valuation could be applied to quoted and unquoted companies.

Let us now summarise our proposed scheme. The method of calculating profit which we recommend begins from the proposition that profit is the difference between the value of the company's own assets at the end and the beginning of the year. To this we add what has left the company in tax and dividend payments, while new capital arising from share issues is deducted. Additional adjustments may be necessary, if, for example, the owners have paid themselves very high salaries as a means of avoiding double taxation. The tax laws allow them to do this, but it cannot be accepted without qualification in relation to the employee funds.

We have dealt in detail with the problems which have to be resolved if company accounts are to serve as a basis both for calculating profits and for valuation. We are convinced that it is desirable and also technically feasible to link the appropriations to the funds to profits, and to link the annual valuation to a valuation of a company's assets and liabilities which is consistent with the profit concept. We accordingly recommend that this idea should be the subject of the most careful examination.

Obviously, both parts of our proposal would require legislation which did not flinch from calling for candour and openness in companies' accounting procedures. Nor, however, is there any question of requiring companies to do anything which would be unreasonable. Many companies which already compile informative sets of annual accounts would find that the changes we are proposing are in fact extremely modest.

(iv) *The rate of allocation of profits*
Apart from the total amount of the profit, the critical factor for the growth of the fund in each particular company is the proportion of profit which is to be appropriated to the fund.

We propose that these appropriations should be made *before* tax, for two reasons. In the first place, this will be advantageous to companies in improving their solvency levels and ensuring that their liquidity at least does not deteriorate. Secondly, the appropriations to the fund will hit the existing shareholders, and the proportion allocated ought not therefore to be made so large that the supply of risk capital could be adversely affected. By exempting them from tax, the size of the appropriations to the funds can be increased and a more rapid rate of growth of the funds can be achieved.

The contributions of capital made by the existing owners will for some considerable time continue to be the main source of supply of new risk capital, although the fourth National Pension Fund can also play an important part. Accordingly, the expected yield on investments made in companies cannot be reduced substantially. Otherwise, capital would shift to other forms of investment which are not affected by the funds or the required rate of return on investments would rise so steeply that the total volume declined.

However, expected yields are not so finely balanced that every change means a decline in the relative propensity to invest in shares. People buy shares for other reasons, for example to obtain greater real protection of their assets than they can achieve via the banks; they may invest in growth stocks in order to reduce their tax liabilities, and so on. We conclude that a modest reduction in the expected yield from shares lies within the margin of uncertainty which applies in any case to profit expectations. A major reduction, on the other hand, would require other forms of investment to be penalised as well, so that capital did not desert the stock market in favour of such things as speculation in land. Lastly, freedom in Sweden to select the profit levels which the country is willing to accept is also limited by her international dependence and by the comparative mobility of capital across frontiers.

In principle, therefore, we propose that appropriations to the funds should be tax-free, in order to combine a modest allocation with a reasonable rate of build-up of the funds. One can of course question whether it is reasonable for the taxpayer to contribute in this way to the accumulation of the employee investment funds; a reduction in tax receipts from one source must presumably be offset by higher tax revenues from another.

It is not clear, however, how the exemption from taxation of the appropriations to funds will in fact hit tax payments by companies. We have already observed that under existing tax legislation companies are very largely able to regulate for themselves how large the profit reported for tax purposes is to be, provided they invest and expand. Companies do not always take advantage of all the opportunities that exist for creating concealed reserves, preferring for a variety of reasons to report larger profits than they need to. In that kind of situation the allocations to employee investment funds could in part be transfers from tax credits, some of which would still exist. There would then be no question, either, of tax payments failing to be made (not, at any rate, if we assume that the firm is growing sufficiently fast that tax credits need not be repaid in the foreseeable future). On the contrary, the tax credit, which under the present system gives neither a return nor any power, would provide both if it were instead to become the employees' own capital.

In other instances the tax-free appropriation to a fund would mean an increase in capital retained within the enterprise and thus an actual reduction in tax payments. It is important to note, however, that this tax exemption would operate in a radically different manner from the generous tax rules which apply at present. The present system provides owners of capital with an increase in the value of their assets, whereas the tax exemption through the funds would accrue entirely to the employee group. If one takes the view that it is too easy for companies to consolidate or that they will gain this facility through the establishment of funds, it would make sense to press for legislation which was less generous in other respects, while exempting from tax the allocations made to the employee funds. By contrast to the two special funds set up in 1974 (for improving the environment at work and for a special investment reserve), the employee investment funds have no negative effect at all on the distribution of wealth.

Weighing up tax exemption and a reduction in the profit expectations of the previous shareholders which is acceptable in the light of the desired level of capital formation, we have arrived at the figure of 20 per cent of profits as a reasonable proportion for allocating to the fund. The rate ought not at all events to be less than that, given our method of valuing a company, which as a rule will involve higher values than the stock market valuations.

Depending on how the yield on the firm's capital varies, or on variations in the relationship between profit and value, as we discussed these concepts earlier, the fund in the individual company will grow in accordance with Table 1.

Table 1 *Employee fund's share of the individual company where profits vary (assuming that 20 per cent of profits is allocated to the fund)*

year	5%	profits 10%	15%	20%
1	0·01	0·02	0·03	0·04
5	0·05	0·09	0·13	0·17
10	0·09	0·17	0·24	0·30
15	0·14	0·25	0·34	0·42
20	0·18	0·32	0·43	0·52
25	0·21	0·38	0·50	0·60
35	0·29	0·49	0·62	0·72
50	0·38	0·62	0·75	0·84
75	0·52	0·76	0·88	0·93
100	0·74	0·85	0·94	0·97

(v) Concerns

All the constituent companies in a combine must be treated as a single entity. One reason for doing this is that we are proposing to exclude small firms from the scope of the system of funds. Firms in a combine might then use this exemption as a loophole, manipulating prices and transferring all their profits to a small member of the group designated for that purpose. Another reason for treating them as an entity is to avoid any tendency to hive off companies for artificial or unwarranted reasons. The profits of the whole concern should serve as the datum for appropriations to the employee fund, and the worth of all the member companies should be determined by the methods which we have already discussed. The employee shares should then be issued in the parent company. For these purposes the concern would include not only subsidiaries in which there was a majority holding, but every enterprise in which the concern held organisation shares.

The position of international companies is rather different. In their case only the profit generated in Sweden should be used as a basis for appropriations to the funds, and the dividends of Swedish companies from foreign subsidiaries should therefore be excluded from the profit used as the base. It then follows that the shares which a Swedish parent company owns in its foreign subsidiaries should not be included in the worth of the parent company. The opposite would apply in the case of Swedish subsidiaries of foreign-owned companies.

In the case of valuations of shares which are not subsidiaries' or organisation shares, consideration should be given simply to omitting them from the scope of the system. They would then be assigned no value and any dividends from them would not be included in profit. The reason for such a rule would be to avoid the toil and trouble of making calculations of profit and worth for other companies of which the constituent companies of the concern perhaps owned only a very modest part. These other companies might in any event be large enough to be covered by the system in their own right. There would of course have to be checks on manipulation, so that 'sister enterprises' which were not part of the same group but nevertheless had a clear community of interest, for example through the same owners or families, could be regarded as a combine. Some form of impartial arbitration should be able to test whether situations of this kind exist in practice.

(vi) *The funds and multinational companies*
A special study of multinational companies and the problems which they can create for the trade union movement was submitted to the 1976 LO Congress. The report argued that,

if Sweden is to come to grips with the problems of companies which invest internationally, economic life must first be made more democratic by ensuring that the community and employees can have a real influence over the major companies.

The establishment of employee funds can be an important element in this process, although the members of LO who took part in the study campaign on employee funds were in no doubt that the multinational companies do present serious problems with regard to economic democracy and employee influence through the funds.

(a) *The multinationals and employment.* In the past ten years there has been a rapid increase in the establishment of Swedish companies abroad. At the same time, foreign companies have shown little interest in setting up business in Sweden except as a means of buying out Swedish companies with a worldwide reputation. This may well continue, and in time give rise to industrial and employment problems in Sweden. The industrial sector may conceivably become too narrow in scope to be able to meet our aspirations for both the public sector and the industrial sector itself. A good illustration of the way in which the international investments of large companies may have an adverse effect on the structure of industry is that foreign purchases of profitable Swedish enterprises have not infrequently led to their research in Sweden being discontinued, followed by the threat of total closure. Swedish companies have sometimes moved their research abroad as well, and this undoubtedly does undermine an important part of the foundation of future industrial employment.

Employees have an interest in preventing this kind of thing from happening, and they can achieve this by acquiring a decisive influence in company boardrooms, for example via share ownership through the employee investment funds. These adverse changes in industrial circumstances can, however, occur extremely rapidly, and they must be checked at an early stage, since their consequences may be difficult to remedy.

Our scheme for the allocation of profits to employee funds means that a considerable period of time will elapse before the funds acquire a majority in companies. This may prove less important in the case of the Swedish multinationals than for foreign-owned Swedish subsidiaries. Even a fairly small holding of shares can provide a position of considerable influence in the larger Swedish companies, because of the diffusion of share ownership. By combining forces at company meetings the present owners can obstruct the rapid build-up of employee influence. Nevertheless, we can probably expect employee influence through the funds to grow rapidly in several Swedish multinationals.

The Swedish subsidiaries of foreign-owned multinational concerns are generally owned 100 per cent by the parent company, which means that it will be a very long time before the funds enable employees to achieve majority holdings in these subsidiaries.

We conclude that the growth of the system of funds will proceed too slowly for it to serve as an active instrument of industrial policy for dealing with the effects which the internationalisation of large companies has on production and employment. These problems will have to be resolved by other methods, as the LO Congress report on multinationals envisaged.

(b) *Abnormally low reported profits in Sweden.* In most multinational concerns, Swedish as well as foreign, the directors can choose the constituent enterprises (and countries) in which to show profits and losses. There is a constant exchange of goods and services between the firms within a concern, and prices can deliberately be fixed too high or too low in this internal trade in order to determine the amount of profit or loss in each of the constituent companies.

Profits are also transferred between the member firms

through the rates of interest fixed for loan transactions within the group. In addition, profits are shifted by means of quite fictional transactions: for example, companies are increasingly being established for the purpose of owning all the patents in a concern, and the other companies pay them for the use they make of patent rights.

It can be very difficult to penetrate profit manipulation of this kind; to counter it some form of rule or trigger mechanism has to be devised which comes into operation whenever low profit levels are reported. One method would be to postulate a standard profit for the Swedish constituent company. This would be the same proportion of the total profit of the group as the Swedish company's share of the total activity of the group (as measured, for example, by the Swedish share of the total manufacturing value of the concern). It should be possible to make this standard rule the principal one. In the light of what we said earlier about the increasing efforts which many enterprises are making, in fact, to report profits where they belong, it is probably simpler and more appropriate to stipulate some guaranteed minimum level of profit as the standard. If it were to fall short of this level a company should be required to justify to independent arbitrators the exceptionally low level of profit in Sweden; otherwise, the standard would automatically apply.

(c) *Swedish subsidiaries of foreign multinationals.* Even if a majority position were to be achieved through the funds in firms belonging to multinational concerns, it would not follow that any real influence over them had been acquired. The power of the multinationals is founded on capital, but backed also by the fact that they control information and large organisations. Foreign-owned multinationals can counter employee influence in individual subsidiaries in Sweden via the funds by virtue of the fact that they do control information and the organisational structure of their Swedish activities.

They can organise production in such a way that the

Swedish subsidiary is required to market its products 'in a package' along with the products of other member firms or through the sales channels of the multinational. This effectively deprives the subsidiary of any opportunity to sell its products itself on the open market.

The dependent status of the subsidiary can also be emphasised by locating product development centrally and giving central management the power to allocate new products, thus making future production in the subsidiary entirely dependent on the investment and production planning of the foreign management for the group as a whole.

Organisationally, several subsidiaries can be established in Sweden, each of which is directly responsible to a foreign member company of the concern, so that the subsidiaries have no legal ownership connection with one another in Sweden. One of the subsidiaries may carry out strategic functions for the others in Sweden, but itself have few employees and little capital. Thus, for example, the other Swedish subsidiaries could be contractually bound to produce certain products which are then sold through the master company, and their dependence on it could be reinforced by this key company carrying out accounting and administrative functions for them on a consultancy basis, or through renting equipment and accommodation which it owns to the other subsidiaries. The master company can in these various ways direct the others and collect the profits which they make.

Foreign-owned firms would have a fair degree of scope for influencing and determining what happened in a Swedish subsidiary which the employee funds dominated, so that the introduction of these funds would hardly be likely to deter foreign firms from setting up in Sweden. Even after the introduction of employee funds, those factors which presently determine the interest, or lack of interest, of foreign companies in their investments in Sweden would still be paramount.

Until the day when employee funds do have a majority shareholding, foreign owners can on the other hand strive to alter the production and organisational structure of Swedish subsidiaries in such a way that the matter of ownership becomes of little moment compared to control over information and organisation. But this process is already in train internationally within the large multinationals, and the picture will not be fundamentally altered by the introduction of employee funds. Legislation and industrial policy measures will have to be deployed to meet the problem. On a long view, the employee funds can improve the bargaining position of the unions. Once they have achieved a majority position in a foreign-owned subsidiary, the employees can, for example, work at developing products and a range of output which are independent of the foreign, previously the parent, concern in order in this way to create a more independent enterprise in the long run.

The system of funds should be constructed in such a way that it covers all the Swedish subsidiaries of a particular foreign concern, irrespective of size and legal owner- ship status, so that it is more difficult for a foreign-owned multinational to escape the growth in employee influence by making organisational changes. All these subsidiaries should be treated as a single unit, and employee representa- tives should have seats on the boards of each one of them to the extent warranted by the funds' holding in the group as a whole.

(d) *Swedish multinationals and the funds.* The employee investment fund system is based on the idea that the employees are to share in the profits which they work to create within Swedish enterprises. The profits generated in the foreign subsidiaries of Swedish multinationals should not be included in the system. Nevertheless, Swedish multinationals have the same opportunities as others to report abroad profits which ought properly to be ascribed to Sweden, so that it is practically impossible to obtain a proper picture of the profit position in these Swedish concerns. As with foreign-owned concerns, therefore, the systematic under-reporting of profits within

Sweden should be countered by specifying some form of standard or control.

Within the separate companies of the Swedish multinationals the chances of exercising influence depend on the group's organisational structure and the control over information. The trend which we noted with reference to foreign-owned multi-nationals is also occurring in their Swedish counterparts, but with one essential difference: the employee investment fund shares will give direct influence in the parent company and therefore over the top management of Swedish multinationals, as long as the parent company and the top management reside in Sweden. Influence is also likely to be acquired more rapidly in the Swedish parent companies than in foreign-owned subsidiaries in Sweden, because of the spread of ownership in the former. This means that the prospects for exercising trade union influence on the Swedish multinational concerns are significantly better than in the case of foreign-owned subsidiaries operating in Sweden.

In isolated cases Swedish multinationals might seek to counter the introduction of employee funds by removing such a large proportion of their production abroad that the residue left in Sweden was insufficient for the company to be covered by the fund system. This is scarcely likely to happen, however, except in the case of occasional small companies. Where it did occur the improved controls over the foreign activities of Swedish companies which is proposed in the report on multi-nationals to the 1976 LO Congress would be brought to bear.

Technically, Swedish multinationals could also subvert the aims of the employee funds by formally altering the company's nationality. A holding company located abroad would take over the ownership of all the companies in the group, including the parent Swedish one. Swedish shareholders would receive shares in the foreign holding company in exchange for their share in the parent company. It would not escape formally in this way from the system of funds; but the ownership in it which the funds acquired would have the same limited opportunities for exercising influence as exists in foreign-owned subsidiaries. Share transactions of this kind would however require official approval, which in all probability the Riksbank would withhold. Such transactions ought in any case to be prohibited.

The introduction of employee funds in Swedish multinationals can give rise to serious difficulties for international trade union solidarity. In step with the growth of influence on the part of funds over the investment, production and employment of Swedish multinationals, both at home and abroad, the Swedish unions would increasingly find that they were in the position of employer *vis-à-vis* their comrades in other countries. The sense of 'our' mutual trade union interests across national frontiers in the face of 'their' multinational enterprises is undoubtedly important for international trade union collaboration to flourish, and it would no longer exist. The Swedish trade union movement must face up to this challenge. Real and imaginary opposition between employees of Swedish subsidiaries abroad and the employees of Swedish concerns must be bridged.

One first step towards this end would be to require that only the profits of the Swedish enterprises within a concern should form the basis for employee fund share allocations. The profits produced by workers in Swedish subsidiaries abroad would be excluded. Yet ownership of shares in a Swedish parent company does provide influence for the unions over a concern both in Sweden and overseas. Developments in Sweden depend on what happens abroad, and vice versa, and it is quite impossible to try to restrict the influence of employee funds in these concerns to 'Swedish' questions, since they frequently cannot be distinguished in this way.

The Swedish unions must accordingly make contact with the unions in Swedish subsidiaries abroad and establish some kind of body to provide for trade union collaboration in which investment trends, production and employment in the various constituent parts of a concern can be discussed. No doubt many awkward situations will occur for the Swedish unions, as for example when Swedish industrial policy interests conflict with the solutions which international trade union solidarity may require. However, these are not problems created by the introduction of employee investment funds. They already exist; but at present they are resolved without any trade union involvement and influence. The difference under a system of employee investment funds is that the employees themselves in different countries assume responsibility for what happens; the matter becomes more democratic.

International trade union solidarity also opens up the prospect that the Swedish unions will have to accept the possible introduction of similar schemes in other countries. This could mean that Swedish subsidiaries in these countries become separated as regards ownership from the Swedish concerns. This need not lead to insurmountable problems provided the problem of international union co-operation within them can be resolved. All that it would mean would be that international economic co-operation was taking place in more democratic forms. Companies in individual countries would come much more under the direct control of those employed within them and at the same time these employees would be establishing new ways of achieving the necessary international economic collaboration. This kind of development is surely in accord with the aspirations of the labour movement.

Chapter 5

The Spread of the System of Funds

In the previous chapter we discussed the method of accumulating the funds out of appropriations from company profits. We shall be concerned in the next chapter with the detailed uses of the income from the funds, but we would stress at this juncture that in fact we propose no formal limit to the beneficiaries from the funds. Every employee, wherever he is employed, should be able to derive some benefit from the system, to take part in administering the funds and to enjoy the fruits of their yield. It is true that there is obviously some limitation, in the sense that it is only the employees of profitable companies who will be able to acquire a direct influence within their own enterprises through the rights which the allocations of shares bring; but we expect that in due course this influence will spill over into a more democratic process pervading the whole of our economic life.

In the present chapter we are concerned particularly with the spread of the funds. What type and size of enterprises should be included in the scheme?

For a variety of reasons the coverage of the funds will have to be confined to certain groups of enterprises. The first reason follows from the construction of the system. If profits are to be used as the basis this means that non-profit-making enterprises, whatever their size and the precise form in which they organise their activities, cannot contribute to the build-up of fund resources. In thinking about other reasons for limiting the coverage of the system it is useful to bear in mind that the appropriateness of the scope of the system has to be judged with regard to (a) objectives, (b) potential benefits to employees and (c) the practical and administrative aspects. Some balance will have to be struck among the three.

We have already discussed the objectives of the system at length. We have seen that there is a dilemma between the need for sustained capital formation on the one hand and the problem of the concentration of wealth and assets which ensues within private industry. In the public sector activities are not pursued for the benefit of a few shareholders; no profit in the normal sense of the term accrues, since the activities such as health, education and transport services are bring provided primarily as a service to the community. There is no increase in private asset holding. Since one of the principal objectives of a system of funds is to counteract an increase of this kind, there is in principle no justification for setting up employee investment funds within the public sector. To transfer public ownership into employee ownership, from the citizens as a whole to a particular group, would be a retrograde step, a kind of 'reprivatisation'. This principle applies whatever the organisational form in which public activity is conducted, whether via administrative agencies, enterprises or publicly owned companies.

Next we must ask whether the objective of countering private ownership and the concentration of wealth provides any guidance as to the position which should be occupied by economic associations which do not aim at individual profit, such as the consumers' co-operative movement. It also aims to counter private asset formation, operating instead on the basis of collective ownership and unrestricted access to membership. This enables every citizen to enter into this collective ownership. The consumer co-operative form of enterprise is an expression of economic democracy, since neither capital nor assets come to be concentrated in the hands of a few. There is as little justification for a gradual transfer of ownership and influence from consumers as a group as we suggested there was for transferring ownership from the people as a whole to employees.

What we have said about consumer co-operatives applies by analogy to other forms of enterprise which are accessible to everyone, which are conducted without the private profit motive, and which have a democratic structure. Various forms of producer co-operative, on the other hand, cannot satisfy the requirement that membership in them is open to everyone, and they cannot advance any arguments in principle for remaining outside the system. The practical solutions to this particular problem will require detailed study, and are beyond our remit.

The forms of enterprise which are to be included in or excluded from the system of funds can in the main be determined on grounds of principle and ideology. The question of the size of enterprise below which no allocation of profit need be made to the system is a much more open one. There is no relationship between size and profitability, so that any size boundary which has to be set for practical purposes is an arbitrary one. On the other hand, one of the arguments for establishing the funds is that they should counteract the concentration of ownership and power in industry, which suggests that only larger companies should be included.

We suggested at the beginning of this chapter that every employee would benefit directly or indirectly from the system, irrespective of whether the company in which he is employed does or does not participate by allocating profits to the scheme. However, employees can only acquire a *direct* influence via co-ownership in firms which do make such allocations out of profits. The membership opinion expressed within LO was very strongly in favour of including every form of enterprise in the system, and the members have similarly favoured the inclusion of small companies as well.

These opinions were expressed in response to an open-ended question, so that no statistical analysis of the responses has been possible. Many LO members see it as a deficiency of the system that employees in firms which are not to be liable to set aside profits to the funds should be denied this avenue of co-ownership as a means of exercising influence on a firm. About 90 per cent of the participants regarded it as absolutely essential or important to give employees ownership rights as a means to increase their influence. It appears that this view also includes enterprises (publicly owned and consumer co-operatives) which in principle or for practical reasons (smaller firms) we wished to exclude. As far as the individual employee is concerned, it is frequently not the type of enterprise but his own position on the job which determines his attitude, and his wishes in this respect are affected very little by whether the business is conducted under public, private or co-operative auspices.

This expression of opinion on the part of LO members must as far as practicable be taken into account in the design of the system of funds. This system cannot be viewed in isolation from other measures aimed at making work more democratic. The fundamental idea in the recent reforms in labour legislation is that labour or work is the wellspring of claims on the part of employees to have some influence over the place in which they spend their working lives. To the extent that this influence can be expanded, and extended to new dimensions, through co-ownership in some sections of the economy, employers in the remaining sectors ought to guarantee a corresponding influence to their employees. In a democracy public activity can never be 'taken over' by its employees; but the public employer can and should be a model employer in the matter of employee influence. The introduction of employee investment funds in the private sector, with the opportunities which it will provide for enhancing employee influence, should be used as an opportunity to review and adjust the legislative rules within the public sector to this new situation. The trade unions in the public sector are of course powerful enough to ensure that this does take place.

We argued earlier that there are good grounds in principle

for excluding the consumers' co-operative movement from the system. This must not, however, be at the expense of employees and their rights to exercise co-influence; nor should they have to forgo any benefit from the resources which the income of the funds has to offer. When we argue for the principle of putting the co-operatives in a special category, we are in fact assuming that alternative solutions will be found which do provide for employee influence, as one element of economic democracy. Some arrangement will also have to be devised to give the employees an equivalent return. (Discussions have been initiated between LO and the Consumers' Co-operative Movement with a view to resolving these problems.)

In addition to the clear-cut categories of ownership which we think should in principle be excluded from the system of funds, there are frequently mixed forms of ownership, such as firms which are jointly owned by consumer co-operatives and private shareholders. An increasingly common mixed form of enterprise is that of private firms with a government stake in them. For mixed forms of enterprise which do contain an element of private ownership the same rules should apply as those for wholly privately owned firms.

The final question about the spread of the system of funds concerns the general size limit. There is a difficult dilemma here, between the strong desire on the part of employees to have their particular firm included and the practical considerations which favour restricting the system to larger firms. We saw that LO members were strongly in favour of including small companies. On the other hand, the technical difficulties clearly increase as one moves down the size scale. It is not even a simple matter to determine a profit concept in large firms with good accounting practices and an open attitude to accountability. These difficulties multiply if smaller firms, frequently with defective accounting practices, are to be included. In many family businesses profit is often taken out in the form of a salary paid to the owner and his family. Additional complications would arise if we were to operate with

73

standards for what is to be regarded as a 'reasonable salary'. The threat of minority interests being introduced into small family enterprises might also encourage them to break up into smaller units. Too low a threshold might also discourage the willingness to establish new enterprise.

Three possible approaches may be suggested by way of a solution to this dilemma. First, size could be combined with total capital employed as a criterion. Companies with a small staff may be quite capital-intensive, and should contribute to the accumulation of the funds. Secondly, the question of association with the system could be made negotiable. If employees in firms below some legally specified size were very anxious to have their company included, they should be able to raise the subject for negotiation. Thirdly, the small firms, whose employees do of course share in the benefits of the proposed system, could be given some priority in the disbursement of the income. We discuss this possibility more fully in the next chapter. Real employee influence is very largely a matter of resources, training and competence. Solidarity among all employees requires that those in small companies should have assigned to them a comparatively large proportion of the common pool of resources.

The practical conclusion to which this whole discussion leads us is that the lower threshold ought not to be below fifty and not above one hundred employees. The size groupings of companies as reported in the 1972 census of companies make little difference to the choice of fifty or one hundred. If the floor were to be set at a hundred employees, 99·2 per cent of firms and 39·9 per cent of employees would fall outside the system, and with a threshold of fifty these figures would be respectively 98·3 per cent and 33·2 per cent.

There are certain types of enterprise which may be termed 'tendentious' or special pleading organisations, such as the newspapers and firms whose objectives are primarily artistic or idealistic in nature. These ought to be dealt with separately. In the present context we are simply sketching the main features of the system, and we do not think that it would be appropriate to take up the extremely complex questions that arise in applying a system of employee investment funds to this type of enterprise. This question, along with others, should be studied by the Royal Commission which is examining the subject of employee influence and capital formation.

One suggestion which the Commission may care to examine is that it should be made possible for enterprises of this type to be conducted as non-profit-making foundations which fall outside the scope of the funds. On the other hand, where the private owners of newspapers and publishers chose to continue to withdraw profits from the enterprises these activities would continue as companies and be covered by the system, as the size of the enterprise determined. Some delimitation would of course have to be made as to the types of activity which could be carried on as foundations; otherwise shell foundations would be set up from which the previous owners proceeded to extract their profits in the form of salary payments.

Chapter 6

Agenda for the Funds

The right of the employer to direct and allocate work is the everyday and manifest expression of a lack of democracy at work and of potential dominance in relation to those who do work. When the subject of increased democracy at the place of work was placed firmly on the agenda some five years ago the abolition of this managerial right, which has been symbolised by the abandonment of 'Paragraph 32', became the prime target. This paragraph was the one in the rules of the Swedish Employers' Confederation (SAF) which has caused so much anguish and controversy as to the employer's management rights. The recent abolition of this right through the 1976 Act on the Joint Regulation of Working Life means that the legal position of the employee has been strengthened, with a view to making it possible for him or her to exercise some real influence over conditions at the place of work. The labour law reforms deal primarily with the internal situation of a firm. The improved status of safety representatives, the rules about the interpretation of agreements, the right to information, and the opportunity to bargain about work organisation and personnel policy – all these illustrate that co-determination is intended in the first instance to apply to those matters which affect everyone intimately in their everyday working life.

The employee investment funds do not deal primarily with these matters. Nor is it the intention that they will assume responsibility for the government's industrial policy. The responsibility for planning the economy should rest with those bodies, the government and the Riksdag, which are responsible to the whole population.

What is specific to the employee funds is that they provide a new opportunity for also making more democratic those decisions which are arrived at within enterprises but which affect a firm's relations with the community as a whole, with consumers, local authorities, the total environment, and so forth. In short, the funds should make it possible to arrive in a democratic manner at those investment decisions which affect what is to be produced and where. Thus it can be argued that the funds would involve a new stratum of democracy in industry, lying somewhere between the two levels that have been attempted so far, government industrial policy on the one hand and the labour law route providing for co-determination within enterprises on the other.

There are obviously no sharp boundaries between these different planes of influence. They intermingle. Nevertheless, it may be meaningful to examine in turn the delimitation of the funds *vis-à-vis* labour legislation and industrial policy, as a means of giving added precision to the agenda for the funds and also obtaining pointers as to their proposed organisation.

The question of how far any extended right of negotiation should stretch featured prominently in the discussion of *labour law reforms*. In their minority report to the original report of the Royal Commission on Labour Law, and later in their formal responses to the proposed legal formulations, the representatives of LO and TCO (the Central Organisation of Salaried Employees) argued that it should be possible to conclude an agreement on *every* topic, including production decisions. One might then think that the precise objectives of the employee investment funds could be achieved via labour legislation. But there is an important difference between the right to negotiate and conclude agreements about production decisions on the one hand, and the influence over production which flows from the ownership of capital on the other. He who controls the capital holds the right to initiate and the chance positively to embark on implementing decisions which are thought to be appropriate. In the last resort he who negotiates can only say 'No'. He cannot press in the same way for particular decisions about proposed ventures if the owner of capital is opposed to committing resources of capital.

This difference, between a positive right to initiate and the possibility of stopping undesirable projects, is illustrated clearly by the fact that the most far-reaching proposal in labour law which has been raised so far concerns a blanket right of veto for the employees, for example over production decisions. Such a right would dramatically strengthen the employees' position. The employer could no longer take on anything which conflicted with their interests. But even if a right of this kind were to be introduced, it is obvious that economic democracy could not be said to have become all-pervasive. The right would remain, in fact, to take decisions as to the size and nature of investments. Labour legislation cannot therefore be a complete proxy for the power over capital which the employee investment funds would provide.

None the less, there are numerous points in common. It is striking that such an overwhelming majority of those who took part in the LO consultations on the funds concluded that the ownership of capital was an essential or very important complement to the labour legislation reforms. The funds would clearly do this in an important way. Just as the right to say 'No' to decisions about production to which one is opposed can be viewed as a necessary if not sufficient step on the road to economic democracy, so can the collective ownership of capital be considered a necessary if still not sufficient condition for the full implementation of the employees' right to determine their own local situation at work. That is how the replies to the first question in the consultative process are to be interpreted. Capital owned by the staff is regarded as guaranteeing that the framework of the new labour legislation can have poured into it a concrete content of far-reaching co-determination. If capital were to be entirely dominated by private interests in the future as well, a quite different situation would exist, in which every extension of employee influence would be at risk the whole time and would perhaps have to be captured anew. The funds would breach the opposition of existing owners to employee influence, because every extension of co-determination which the employees achieved would lead to a corresponding loss of power and influence on the part of the present owners.

The funds can reinforce the labour legislation reforms quite crucially in one other respect as well. The consultative process provided strong support for the idea of utilising the income from the funds for collective purposes, supporting these very activities of employee representation on boards, broader negotiating rights, improved status for safety representatives, and so on.

When we turn to the relations between the funds and *industrial policy* we have already made the obvious first point, that the government and Riksdag ought to have the over-riding responsibility for industrial policy. On the other hand, concrete investment decisions are hardly the job of government bodies, now or in the future. Government industrial policy ought to comprehend guidelines and plans for the broad sweep of development, for steering investment towards areas of high unemployment and away from overheated regions. It should seek to achieve a sufficient volume of investment to maintain a competitive industrial structure. It should be responsible for development work in sectors which have been given social priority. It should seek to ensure that manufacturing processes are sensitive to the environment both outside and inside plants. The mechanisms of control which it deploys may be gentle or firm, depending on the importance of the question and the kind of response which government planning evokes. But scarcely anyone imagines that it would become customary for the state to intervene and make the specific decisions. The vision of future government industrial policy embraces the strategic planning which will increasingly be required to ensure jobs for all and the growth of essential production, while utilising production methods which do not make excessive demands on the environment and on the stock of resources. What it does not comprehend is a planned economy on the pattern which exists today primarily in the Eastern European states.

Industrial policy would then be limited in scope as well, as long as industry continued to be dominated by private capital. Specific decisions can be affected by the negative device of a ban, though this policy instrument has rather a narrow range of usefulness. The technique of prohibition may be used to protect particularly sensitive environmental areas, as a means of preventing production which is directly harmful, and so on. But prohibitions can hardly be used on a large scale as a means of achieving what is actually wanted without at the same time putting at risk positive and essential production decisions.

Incentives provide a more positive control mechanism. The government can nudge private decisions in the direction favoured by its political objectives by offering inducements such as tax concessions, investment grants, location subsidies and training grants. But although they can be a more useful stimulus than a direct ban, even incentives have a fairly restricted range of usefulness. If they are to persuade firms to arrive at different decisions, economic incentives must be strong enough for the expected rate of return on the new decision to exceed the expected profit on the previous un-influenced decision. The implication is that incentives augment profits and the accumulation of assets in the hands of owners of capital. As long as these consist mainly of a handful of private persons there is a conflict between the call for greater equality in the distribution of ownership and the desire to persuade decisions in a particular direction. Under the existing structure of ownership, therefore, economic incentives can only be used on a modest scale. They can quickly become costly and involve some major redistributions from the multitude of taxpayers to the few who own capital. The employee investment funds can accordingly have a value of their own in connection with government policy towards industry.

In the last resort it is the totality of all individual investment decisions which companies take that determines industry's future. One can assume that the over-riding objective of industrial policy will be comprehended quite differently from the present system in companies which come to be dominated by employee funds. Quite the most obvious difference will be that social and private employment objectives will largely coincide. In the purely private enterprise, employment has no value in its own right; rather the reverse. It is true that the freedom of employers to dismiss staff without let or hindrance is limited by the legislation on security of employment, notice of redundancy, and so on; and many firms do demonstrate a considerable degree of responsibility towards those they employ. Nevertheless, fewer staff employed means lower costs for the firm. The higher social costs which the community as a whole may have to bear are not something that the firm need take into account. Private companies can therefore use employment as a kind of 'hostage' or pressure against the community. (This is not to pass judgement on the morality or otherwise of such behaviour; it is simply a fact of life in an economy in which business profit is the supreme criterion in decision making.)

In the employee-dominated economy, on the other hand, there is the basis for greater accord between the community and the company, and firms can be expected to be more sensitive to the needs of industrial policy. The community also becomes more free to deploy economic incentives if the fruits do not accrue to a few private capitalists but to employees as a whole.

As a matter of fact, the introduction of employee investment funds would greatly strengthen the prospects for sustaining and developing the market economy in areas where it functions well. It should be easier in an employee-dominated economy to bring a firm's decisions into harmony with social objectives without the community having therefore to step in and control the various decisions in detail.

Thus the employee investment funds have their own job to perform, both in relation to worker influence at the local level and to the comprehensive tasks of industrial policy. There is therefore no conflict between pressing simultaneously for reforms in labour legislation aimed at strengthening the position of labour in relation to that of capital, for a stronger government industrial policy, and for the introduction of employee investment funds. On the contrary, it will be for the funds to enhance the legal status of the worker and at the same time support overall industrial policy. This will be possible because of the two main duties which will fall to the funds: administering the income from the portfolio of shares, and representing the funds' shareholders at board level.

THE FUND INCOME AS A MEANS OF ASSISTING LOCAL
EMPLOYEE INFLUENCE

One of the fundamental conditions of our proposed system is that the collective capital of the funds must not be consumed. Any departure from this requirement would imply that the capital was either being consumed or returned to the previous owners, and that would of course be contrary to the object of transferring part of the growth in capital to the employees as a group.

The yield on the capital of the funds, i.e. the dividends on the total share capital, can be likened to the rebates which consumer co-operatives disburse. These can be disposed of freely by the members, and used for consumption or saving as the individual chooses. But just as the co-operative rebate is determined only after a proportion of the profit has been earmarked for new investment, so must part of the yield on the funds be reserved for the purchase by the fund of new issues of shares. Companies sometimes turn to their shareholders, and have increasingly done so of late, to obtain new capital; to finance new investment on too large a scale via borrowing would lead to a worsening of the equity/debt ratio (solvency level) of companies. The employee funds must be able, indeed eager, to participate in these new issues, otherwise their proportion of the total share capital would decline or at any rate grow more slowly. We therefore assume that the employee investment funds will make full use of their rights to subscribe to new issues of shares.

For some years new issue activity in Sweden has been decidedly modest, amounting to 200 m.–300 m. crowns a year, while the requirements of capital by companies have been several times larger, if they wished to preserve some desired relationship between their own capital and borrowings. New issue activity did, however, gather pace in the course of 1975, and it is likely to remain substantial over the next few years, having regard to future investment requirements. It is likely that the fourth National Pension Fund will be able to contribute an increasing share of this risk capital, but the employee funds must for their part ensure that they safeguard their own growth prospects. It is not unrealistic to assume that half of the yield accruing to the funds will be required to finance the purchase of new shares arising from new issues.

It is in the allocation of the remaining half between reinvestment, private consumption or collective consumption that some choice is possible. Reinvestment can take various forms, such as the purchase of shares either in one's own firm or through the market, investment in pension funds or banks, supporting weak industries or acquisitions of companies. A remarkable number (nearly 14 per cent of those who commented at all, and over 6 per cent of the total) of those who participated in the study campaign in the autumn of 1975 proposed some of these alternatives, although they were not mentioned in the study material which was distributed. Share purchases were the most popular alternative, and it appears from the answers that what people most frequently had in mind was joint purchases by the employees in a firm and, less frequently, purchases of shares by individuals. There were also many advocates of the idea that the income should be used to support weak enterprises. A vote in favour of reinvesting income in some of the ways indicated is comparable to the choice which the individual member of a consumers' co-operative makes when he refrains from withdrawing his rebate for direct consumption. There is clearly a substantial body of opinion among the members in favour of utilising the income from the funds for industrial policy purposes.

However, the main alternatives among which the participants in the study campaign were asked to choose related to the question of whether the income should be used for collective purposes or for making disbursements in cash to employees. Even bearing in mind that the former alternative was recommended in the study material, the views of the members must be regarded as unequivocal, in that no fewer than 94 per cent of the total wished to see the income used in some collective manner.

The yield on the funds should benefit all employees, irrespective of where they are employed, in large or small enterprises, in private or public activity. It can and should be an instrument of trade union solidarity.

Our study material instanced four examples of possible uses to which the income could be put: (a) education in business economics and political economy, (b) support for safety at work, (c) research and development in work organisation and (d) support for the adjustment teams set up to assist older and handicapped workers. The participants were asked to indicate themselves additional examples of uses for the available income, and they readily did so. Comments on this point accounted for no less than half the total comments reported. We can therefore say with some justification that the question of the utilisation of the income aroused considerable interest among those members who were interested in the study material. Table 2 indicates how the comments can be grouped roughly into categories in response to Question 3 of the study material.

Table 2   *Suggested uses for fund income*

	%
Education in business economics and political economy	26
Safety at work (including health services)	13
Research and development in work organisation	4
Support for adjustment teams	4
	47
Purchases of shares	13
Support for weak firms and other measures of industrial policy	13
Recreational facilities	7
Social benefits	7
Reductions in union dues	4
Cultural activities	3
Other proposals	6
	53
Total	100

These results are not to be interpreted as meaning that the majority of the members gave a lower priority to the alternatives suggested in the study material which was distributed. It can be assumed that many of those who put forward no proposals of their own considered that these alternatives were appropriate ones. But it is quite obvious that there is a strong body of opinion in favour of utilising the income for industrial policy purposes. During a fairly lengthy period of build-up the yield will not be large enough to permit worthwhile efforts along these lines. However, we shall demonstrate in the next section that industrial policy in a certain sense can be pursued within the framework of the proposed system of funds, and that this can be done not merely with the help of the income but via the increase in the influence which employees will in due course come to have over management decisions. It is important to keep in mind the expression of membership opinion on this point in constructing the fund system.

All the proposals for the uses to which the income should be put share the view that they should be devoted to supporting local union activities, and not be used to reduce the obligations that normally rest on other groups, in particular companies and the community at large, to support such things as education, research, and the industrial and social responsibilities of the community. Safety at work, personnel policy and company health schemes are the kind of activities which fall to companies. Trade union resources ought not in principle to be utilised for such purposes. But the unions, particularly local branches, do require large resources if they are to be able to play an active part in all those areas in which they are demanding greater efforts from the community and from companies, but in which positive results can only be achieved if the union, i.e. the members themselves, can be made to take an active interest and become knowledgeable and competent. Local unions should take stock of the numerous problems in the workplace, formulate demands for action by the community and by companies, ensure practical and aggressive application of the content of agreements and legislation, and safeguard the interests of their members in every situation and on all the levels to which the labour legislation reforms give them formal entitlements. Legislation and the texts of agreements only provide the framework; whether they are to be given living content is a matter of will, membership activity and, above all, of resources.

The community and business firms should be responsible in part for furnishing these resources. But it is an inestimable advantage if the trade union movement itself can manage to mobilise a significant share of the resources and dispose of them as it thinks best. It is no accident that the members gave pride of place to matters of education. The existing range of commitments of the trade union movement already makes great demands of trade union education, not for a slender cadre of union officials but for large groups of members. In fact the most effective counter to any bureaucratic tendencies in the unions and the best way of reducing the gap between elected officers and other members is via a broadening of this educational activity, and also by allowing union duties to circulate among the many, and in general increasing union activities. The vitality and bargaining strength of a trade union movement depend on membership activity, and that in turn depends to a high degree on the knowledge and competence of the members. Moreover, we are now at the beginning of a new phase, where employees have wrested for themselves the right to exercise a real influence within companies. These reforms have been met by two sorts of criticism. One, coming mainly from employers, claims that the reforms in labour law will cause uneasiness, unwieldy decision-making processes, and inefficiency in industry; the other, distrusting all reform, claims that in reality there is little to be gained by employees and that the reforms will remain paper tigers. Despite their apparently different sources, these criticisms have one thing in common, namely, a lack of confidence in the capacity of trade union members to master these new responsibilities.

The educational tasks ahead are manifold. The participants in the study campaign gave priority to business economics and political economy. Many union members who have had experience as members of company boards feel that their contribution has been inadequate. Others consider that the labour legislation reforms will make major demands on their trade union skills in these areas. Many declare that a system of employee funds will stand or fall with the prospects for raising the level of education among those who one day will assume part of the functions of ownership. Thus it is very important to devote more intensive efforts to the educational work which has already been launched for those members who are to be concerned with implementing the labour law reforms. The old saying, 'Knowledge is Power', is a truth that appears increasingly self-evident when the new labour law comes to be applied in practice.

The unions are already short of employee consultants who are meant to provide expertise in support of union representatives on boards of directors. The need for expertise of various kinds will grow in step with the implementation of the reforms in working life. The prospects of the unions recruiting people for this purpose are rather limited, and could be broadened if the employees were themselves to establish educational institutions with their own resources. There is in Sweden a business school which is principally financed through private donations. The unions do not need to establish a similar institution in order to satisfy their own training aims, but it does not appear to be unreasonable to envisage that the specialists who will in future provide support for employee interests on boards should receive part of their training under union auspices.

There is a similar argument in favour of a trade union initiative in research and investigation work. Most of the research in business economics and political economy is carried out in government institutions and with public money. But private industry does finance a significant amount of research, for example through the Industrial Institute for Economic and Social Research (IUI), which deals mainly with long-term problems. Other research projects are financed by the Industry and Society Studies Group (SNS). A lot of fundamental and contract research in business economics is carried out at the Economic Research Institute of the business school in Stockholm. The Swedish Employers' Confederation finances a special research institute for personnel administration studies.

The above list is incomplete, and it is not intended as an attack on industrially sponsored research; but it does demonstrate how utterly passive the labour movement is in this key area. It is illusory to imagine that research can be free from value judgements. Research methods are, or should be, free of value judgements, but not the choice of research projects. The unions should abandon their passive attitude in this field now that they are on the way to acquiring a new standing in working life.

Educational problems also loom large in considering more resources for union activities dealing with safety at work and the working environment. The main responsibility for the environment at work does not lie with the trade union movement. Nevertheless, the nature and effectiveness of activity in this area are heavily dependent on union action. Regulations about the working environment can only determine minima and set thresholds. More resources are required to provide safety representatives with qualified training, to enable them more readily to take the initiative in necessary measurement and investigative work, and to give them the support of special expertise. The yield from the employee funds should not be used to relieve industry and the community of the burden of duties which rests on them. But the capability of union members and their local representative officers should be increased, so that they can be both vigilant and knowledgeable in working for a good environment and keep a continuing watch on this evolving subject, while pressing also for an improved environment at work. The income from the funds can possibly be used to provide better information, service and consultancy at the sector level, particularly for the benefit of people employed in small firms.

For some years now adjustment teams have been at work in firms throughout the country endeavouring on the basis of tripartite co-operation to find ways of facilitating the employment of older and handicapped workers. This is an important trade union mission, and the union members of these groups should have access to better training and expertise. These teams can be viewed as one strand in developing more direct influence on personnel policy on the part of employees, and it is therefore essential that employees should also be given the resources to cope with these new undertakings.

Most of the remaining suggestions for deploying the income from the funds concerned individual benefits, such as improved recreation facilities. While education and research have to be managed centrally if they are to be effective, this last proposal is one which can best be determined locally. The same applies to cultural activities. Quite a significant number of people mentioned this, when one bears in mind that it was not touched upon in the study material. In many quarters of the labour movement the commercialisation of culture is felt to be profoundly unsatisfactory. Neither the community nor the labour movement itself does enough in this field. Various kinds of cultural activity could with modest resources be undertaken to meet the wishes and needs of members at their places of employment. In some plants there have been experiments with libraries and lending of works of art. Art exhibitions, music and theatre groups could be organised in conjunction with the workers' educational associations. If these activities were linked to the workplace they would also reach people who have traditionally been placed, or placed themselves, beyond this consumption of culture. If part of the yield of the funds were to be used for the purpose of injecting vitality into trade union cultural activities this would also release energies for making the workplace more democratic.

All these possible uses for the income of the funds which we have mentioned so far are an expression of solidarity within the totality of employees, meaning as they do that resources that have been earned in profitable enterprises are disbursed for the benefit of employees throughout the whole economy. This solidarity can and should be strengthened further in one important direction: that of the solidarity between the employees of large firms, who in many respects are favoured by social and labour legislation and also negotiated agreements, and those working in small companies who are left outside. The employee funds system must not in addition become a part of what one union leader has described as a move in the direction of First and Second Division teams within the trade union movement, with solidarity fading in consequence. It is repugnant to think that a proposal whose ultimate objective is that of strengthening trade union solidarity could end up enfeebling it.

Most of the legislative enactments dealing with working life penalise small firms by setting thresholds for their application at a minimum number of employees, usually fifty or one hundred. To put this point in perspective, just over 4,000 firms in Sweden, or 1·7 per cent of the total of some 250,000 enterprises, had more than fifty employees in 1972. A threshold of fifty applies under the Safety at Work Act to the appointment of safety committees, while the experimental legislation on employee directors applied only to companies with more than a hundred employees (reduced in 1976 to twenty-five employees). Similar limits are contained in the agreements concluded by the central labour market organisations. Employees can demand that a Works Council be established only in firms with at least fifty employees, and as a result small firms cannot set up economic committees or appoint employee consultants. Information and trade union education work also encounter greater difficulties in small firms than in others.

So far we have only discussed small and large *companies* or *firms*, but whatever the size of the firm the small *workshop* or *establishment* usually gives rise to various special problems. The building industry is a good example of this, for it is an industry in which workers are frequently employed on small projects of short duration. The financial resources for regional safety representatives in the industry are considered inadequate to cope with the work on a continuing, preventative and regulatory basis in the smaller workplaces. Adjustments teams cannot be linked to companies, but instead there are building worker boards, whose activities are hampered by the large proportion of small establishments. It is also difficult in practice to apply the legislation on educational leave and training of trade union officers to small places of work. Some of these circumstances are peculiar to the building industry, but others are similar in other industries with small workplaces.

It is not in the least surprising that membership opinion was critical of the idea that a system of employee investment funds should operate with similar size limitations. We have already noted that many participants wanted to lower the minimum size below fifty employees, and a further significant number wanted to include every enterprise irrespective of size.

The accumulation of funds has to be restricted to firms of a certain minimum size for practical reasons. This means that in the remainder the formal possibility of employees acquiring influence via co-ownership goes by default. Drawing the boundary line in this way means that the same categories of employees who are already at a disadvantage in other reforms of working life, both legal and negotiated, continue to suffer a disadvantage. All the more reason, therefore, for giving preference in the use of the funds to benefiting employees in small firms. They should be allocated a disproportionately large share of the total income so that they can strengthen their union resources and become better equipped to acquire for themselves the various improvements made via the reforms. The extra resources should accordingly be used to improve training and the working environment, for more intensive work in support of adjustment teams, for better information, and so forth. To some extent these activities should help the owners of small firms as well. One interview study into the educational and training requirements of small businessmen indicated that they themselves consider that their training needs are greatest in the area of legislation and agreements relating to union matters and personnel questions. Those interviewed considered that the training available at present is far too theoretical and directed at the problems of large companies. Both parties should benefit if small businessmen are able to take part to some extent in the trade union training activities. If they become better informed and more knowledgeable, for example about the environment at work, this can lead to improved working conditions.

Exactly how the funds are to be disbursed is a practical question. The essential point is that a substantial proportion of the profits of larger companies should be devoted to increasing the resources available for making small businesses more democratic. In that way the employee investment funds become an expression of solidarity between different groups of employees.

COMPREHENSIVE TASKS FOR THE FUNDS

For a variety of reasons it is not possible at this stage to formulate in a concrete form the more far-reaching tasks which will fall to the funds. In the first place, a lot of water will have flowed under the bridge before the ownership of the funds is large enough for us to be able to speak of a fundamental shift of power which does make possible comprehensive decision making. Circumstances and needs will be changing all the time. Decisions taken through the funds will also depend on how official policy towards industry takes shape. The precise structure of the comprehensive duties of the funds will accordingly be a topic that emerges in step with the growth of the funds.

Some reflections may nevertheless be in order. The funds will exercise their influence through representation on boards of directors. The board is the governing body of the individual company. Thus it is not self-evident that decisions taken there are comprehensive in the sense that they take account of outside interests – for instance those of consumers, the whole industry, local authorities, and so on. The prime duty of the board is to safeguard the interests of the enterprise. If we wish to allocate more comprehensive duties to the employee investment funds, therefore, their organisation has to be built up accordingly.

We have already stressed that the policy of solidarity in wages is fundamental to the Swedish unions. A system of funds in Sweden must not operate in such a way that market forces are again given greater scope in wage determination. The closing of wage differentials has been a welfare gain of decisive significance, and it must not be lost. Company board members who are appointed on the basis of the funds' share of capital ought therefore to be responsible to a wider constituency-of employees than those working in the enterprise. If they were responsible only to their own company group of employees the principle of wage solidarity would in the long run inevitably be at risk. The pressure to extract what one could for one's own group could in many instances become irresistible.

In other respects as well, a pronounced local worker emphasis could be expected to promote a more self-centred system, with perhaps even tougher competition in markets than prevails under the existing system. We should not underestimate the collaboration and planning of structural change which a few dominant groups of owners are able to achieve in Sweden. True, this takes place in the interests of private capital, but despite that we can probably assume that it is less chaotic than a more atomistic free market system.

The very concept of planned structural change can serve as a starting-point for some reflections on the future all-embracing tasks for the funds. Amid all the uncertainty surrounding the distant future in which the funds will be functioning, one prediction can be made with certainty, namely, that the real world that surrounds us will be constantly in flux. Adjustments to new circumstances are never achieved once and for all. They occur and recur. Foreign markets change, the trend continues to an increasingly highly productive industrial sector which requires fewer employees, the age composition of the population alters, and with it the needs of the people. Tastes change, needs become saturated, and so on. The apparatus of production has to adjust. In the unbridled market economy change frequently strikes ruthlessly and hard, particularly at those who are employed in industries and firms which lose their markets.

Anticipating change, finding alternative products, planning for and carrying through the necessary closures, and developing new and viable products for which there is a demand – all of these provide opportunities to adapt the steady process of structural change to people's basic need for work and welfare.

Change itself also carries within it the seed of possible improvements in the environment of work, although such improvements are by no means the inevitable fruit of change. The technological changes which have resulted from the severe alterations in economic structure of the past twenty-five years are clear testimony to the fact that an improvement in the environment at work was in no sense one of the objectives of the changes. The improvements which nevertheless have been made may often appear to have been fortuitous, a byproduct of a general improvement in the performance potential of equipment and organisations. At the same time new environmental problems have been permitted to develop on a scale which is probably still largely an unknown quantity, at least in the sphere of chemicals. Planned changes in the structure of industry which are being pursued by employees must incorporate the rigid stipulation that improvements in the working environment are a keystone of change.

One guiding principle for funds in discharging their more comprehensive duties is that they should collaborate with the official bodies dealing with industrial policy. One can imagine the extra effectiveness which present industrial policy would have if its intentions were in fact translated into action by company boards of directors. It should be possible to develop an interplay between official policy towards industry and the claims of employees which they formulate on the basis of their new experiences in productive life, and this interplay can in addition hold out the prospect of further fruitful developments in the future.

Chapter 7

The Structure and
Administration of the Funds

We have already rejected a design for the funds which is
confined to the individual company. Under such a system the
cohesion which could develop in the small group would
threaten to undermine the solidarity of the larger totality of
employees. Comprehensive funds are needed if every employee
is to be able to obtain a share of the income as well as of the
economic influence which a system of funds can provide. On
the other hand it is also the case that the people who work in an
enterprise do have a legitimate special interest in it, which
warrants their having a proportionately greater influence over
the decisions of their own firm than people who are less directly
involved.

ADMINISTERING THE INCOME

If the income or yield from the system is to benefit all employees
there is only one solution: a central clearing fund to which all
the income is channelled.

The majority of those who took part in the LO consultative
process and responded to this question also expressed the view
that the income should be administered entirely by a central
fund. Ten per cent voted for regional and 5 per cent for
sector funds, while only 6 per cent preferred that funds should
be linked to the individual company. Of the 29 per cent who

proposed combinations of different systems, 22 per cent preferred a combination which included a central fund.

It is clear then that the idea of funds linked to the firm has little support as far as administering the income is concerned. This is regarded as a task for a larger group than a firm's own employees. Many comments in the replies expressed the view very clearly that people wish to see the income used in common, in the first instance for training, for supporting improved working environment and for certain industrial policy activities. The suggestion that the income should be used in support of local employee influence, an idea which evoked a strong and sympathetic response among the members, does not prevent, but indeed requires, that the resources of the funds should be centrally administered.

REPRESENTATION ON BOARDS OF DIRECTORS

The other main task of the funds is to nominate members of boards, and in this respect there is more freedom of choice as regards the level of organisation. It can even be argued that if the central clearing fund were also to nominate board members this would amount to an unnecessary and excessive degree of centralisation. This view found support in the consultative process. A majority favoured a central clearing fund to administer the income, but only 11 per cent wanted to have the central fund nominate board members. The alternative to board representation which attracted most votes was regional funds, with 34 per cent, followed by sector funds, with 17 per cent. Together with those who recommended a combination of central, regional and/or sector funds, an overwhelming majority, 70 per cent, therefore wanted board representatives to be nominated by some kind of more comprehensive funds. Twenty-seven per cent wanted board members to be nominated by company funds. As the question was framed, one can assume that these replies express a general stipulation that the system of funds must not be constructed in such a way that it encourages company or group egoism. The weight of opinion in favour of regional funds can likewise be viewed, in the light of the formulation of the question, as an expression of a recommendation in favour of joint solutions which give some representation on boards to groups of employees who are not directly affected by the system of funds in their own enterprises.

On the other hand, the variations in the replies to both questions are also proof of a desire on the part of the members to have elections taking place nearer the members than in the case of the administration of the funds. The fear of domination by bigwigs and of direction from on high is very forcefully expressed. True, only a small minority, some 8 per cent of those who commented along with the replies to the questions that were posed, expressed such fears. It is, however, obvious, and the point has emerged not least in the course of the information campaign which was arranged during the autumn of 1975, that the fear of rule from the top and the stipulation that board members should be nominated locally should be given considerable weight. In any case there is a clear expression throughout of the view that it is important to have employee influence strongly underpinned at the local level. More than 90 per cent took the position that the local union club must always have the right to nominate when representatives on boards of directors are to be selected.

In our judgement the construction of the funds must respond to the need to associate the system closely with local questions of co-determination as well as with more all-embracing structural issues. Individual employees must be able to feel that their particular funds are part of the process of making their own particular workplace more democratic. Equally, every employee must also experience the funds as part of the process of making decisions about economic change more democratic.

One democratic check which could prevent administration from being carried on over the heads of individual employees would be a *mutual right of veto*, by which local unions and regional or sector funds had to be in agreement about appointments to boards. But we should like to go a step farther, in a direction suggested to us by the membership opinion as expressed in the consultative process.

During the phase when the funds are being built up, they could well operate mainly to strengthen co-determination and rather less as a vehicle for influencing economic progress. We infer from this that, to begin with, any board members should be chosen by the local organisation, which is best placed to assess those matters pertaining to co-determination which should be pursued within the individual enterprise. In due course, when the holdings in most large companies are bigger, the prospects of influencing economic developments will change, and more comprehensive funds should then enter the picture. We therefore propose that the local plant unions should themselves appoint the number of board members warranted by the first 20 per cent of the share capital of a company, and they would have the right to do this at a company's annual meeting. For additional board places to which subsequent share acquisitions entitled them the local plant unions would have the right to make nominations and also a right of veto, but the right actually to make the appointments should rest with a more comprehensive fund.

SECTOR FUNDS

It is a nice question whether such an intermediate fund should be organised on a sector or a regional basis. Many of the issues in which the funds could participate, such as market knowledge, product development and job environment problems, are very heavily focused on the sector or industry. Some form of organisation by sector is therefore desirable in order to ensure the proper collaboration and perspective on such topics. Indeed, employees will need to be equipped to deal with these matters if in due course they are themselves to control the changing structure of industry instead of simply being its victims or agents. From the very launching of the system of funds, therefore, provision should be made for establishing industrywide consultative and advisory bodies – what we call *sector funds*.[1]

To start with these bodies should mainly serve as a resource base for company directors who are appointed by the local trade unions. It may be of enormous significance to them to be able to have recourse to qualified expertise if they are to have a chance of exercising an influence on decisions in the interests of the staff. Issues such as the working environment and work organisation are closely intertwined with co-determination, and valuable contributions on these subjects can be made from the outset. The existing employee representatives on boards of directors should obviously be given access to this expertise as well.

As these sector organisations become knowledgeable about their industry and as the funds gradually acquire more shares and greater influence, they should concern themselves more intimately with the commercial side of the industry, so that they can make a significant contribution to its future development. We also take the view that these sector funds ought to be the agencies which appoint board members when shareholdings in a company come to exceed 20 per cent of the issued capital.

From being at the beginning simply advisory and consultative bodies, the sector funds will gradually become more involved in decision making. They ought not, however, to be regarded as a kind of parent company in a concern; the participating companies should have much more independence than that! One of the tasks for the sector funds will be to assemble expertise and information which are significant for the growth of the sector in the context of government industrial policy. In that capacity they can function as a base organization and support system for members of boards, whose appointment is also one of their duties.

---

[1] These sector funds are not to be confused with the branch funds and branch rationalisation funds which we discussed in Chapter 2, and which were intended as a device for reinforcing the policy of wage solidarity.

Union members and union organisations will certainly put forward suggestions on all kinds of matters, and national unions and LO Congresses will debate and approve action programmes. These cannot bind the sector funds in any formal sense. Naturally, the representatives appointed to sector funds will be elected on these platforms and in practice they will therefore be committed to work for their implementation. In this manner the representative democracy of the unions, which has its roots in the individual union member, will be able to influence the activities of the sector funds.

These sector funds will none the less be independent bodies, and their membership will be drawn from various quarters. Members ought not to be appointed solely from among the unions directly affected; other employees, for example those in central and local government, who do not work in the companies covered by the system of funds, have every right to demand some say about the development of the economy. There should therefore be some representation of the public interest on these sector funds. The community will not of course pursue its national policy *through* the sector funds, since it has other weapons of industrial policy at its disposal. We can however anticipate intensive collaboration between official industrial policy and the employee investment funds, and this process will be facilitated by having publicly appointed members on the sector funds.

It should be possible in sector funds with this wide representation to devise general guidelines for board representation in the firms in an industry which do take account of the interests of the whole aggregate of employees in a broad sense. This should also help to counter any narrow self-interest on the part of an industry and the firms in it.

The sector funds ought accordingly to include one or two public members. Half the remaining members should be appointed by the unions directly interested, probably through their Congresses, and other unions should appoint the remaining half of the union representatives.

It will be seen that we have preferred an industrial or sector basis to a geographical form of organisation, despite the fact that a regional form of organisation attracted most support in the soundings taken via the consultative process (though the margin over sector funds was not a large one). Our main reason for this preference is that co-operation organised on an industrial basis is more likely to reap the benefit of planned changes in industrial structure. Paradoxically, too, it is only by *not* organising on a regional basis that a policy of moderating regional disparities can be pursued. The major environmental issues also tend to be industrial in their emphasis. In addition to that, the alternative which was posed in the consultative process was formulated in such a way that a preference for regional funds became at the same time a choice for giving every employee some influence, and not simply those working in a particular industry. We have endeavoured in our design to satisfy the claim that everyone should have some influence. The regional element need not be lost to view, however, because the circumstances of the employee investment fund system ought also to be taken into account at regional level, particularly in regional planning. The employee representatives on company boards of directors in a region ought to be members of the consultative bodies which are involved in county planning. These bodies should prove to be a very useful source of information about the economy of a region.

THE ORGANISATION OF EMPLOYEE INVESTMENT FUNDS — A SUMMARY

All dividends are paid into a central equalisation or clearing fund, which administers and allocates this dividend income in the various ways we have discussed. At the beginning, before the stage has been reached when the system has begun to generate an entitlement to representation on company boards of directors, this will be the only fund organisation. It may also be appropriate for the national unions to appoint directly the directors of the clearing fund. Smaller unions and those with many small firms in their jurisdictions should be over-represented. A majority of the LO members who expressed a view on the question recommended that the central fund should have on it representatives of the public interest. As we have designed the scheme, however, the sole function of the central fund will be to administer the income from the employee-owned shares, and the allocation of this income is so much a domestic matter for the unions that we refrain from proposing any such public interest representation in the clearing fund.

When the employee investment fund has gradually built up large enough shareholdings to entitle it to representation on the boards of companies, the local unions will appoint the number of company board members to which they are entitled by the first 20 per cent of the total issued capital of the company. Industrywide or sector funds will be set up as a means of providing support and services for these locally appointed board members. In addition to these support and advisory services, the sector funds will gradually come in addition to appoint the additional board members to which the employees are entitled when the fund holds more than 20 per cent of the issued capital. The public interest will be represented in these sector funds. Half the union representation in the sector funds should be allocated to the unions which organise employees in the sector, and half to other unions. On a regional basis, employee representatives on company boards ought to consult and keep in touch with one another and with the regional planning authority.

The scheme is summarised in Figure 2.

As always happens when an allocation is made on the basis of some principle, there will be problems of demarcation. Many companies operate in several industries. Others have subsidiaries in different industries. In such cases different sector funds could appoint representatives according to a system of 'demarcation agreements' based on experience from trade

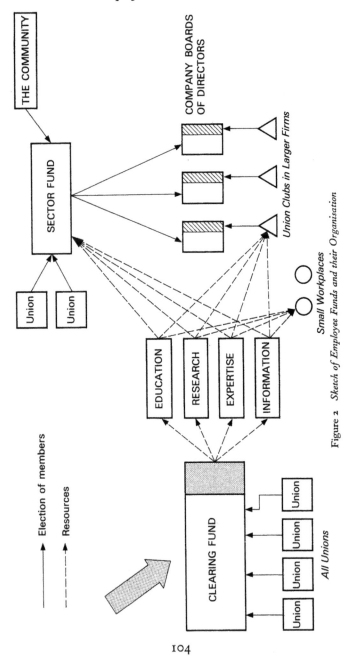

Figure 2   *Sketch of Employee Funds and their Organisation*

union organisation work. The possibility that board members from different sector boards might serve on the same company board and that a company board appointed by *one* sector fund should permit *another* sector fund to appoint representatives to a subsidiary would indicate clearly how the system differs in character from that of regular companies in a concern. The employee investment funds are not the keystone in an organisation which has legitimacy conferred upon it by the rules in the Companies Act regarding the rights of the owners to make decisions. They are instead components in a democratically structured scheme for running the economy.

Chapter 8

The Prospects of Success

In the introductory chapter we indicated the aims of a system of employee investment funds as these can be interpreted from our Congress directive and the underlying discussion. We supplemented that statement of objectives with a brief examination of the conditions which a system of funds has to satisfy if it is not to hamper the achievement of other social objectives. We have rejected a number of methods because they did not meet these conditions, and we eventually arrived at a specific design for employee funds. This design probably suffers from numerous deficiencies; it is based on value judgements which not everyone shares; and, in particular, it is not suited or intended to solve more than a few problems. The employee funds system is to be viewed as one part of a comprehensive work of reform, as one of the many instruments deployed by democratic socialism for steadily creating a better society for the majority of the people. Since we have described such a system as specifically as we can, it may now be worth asking whether it really does match up to the prescribed aims. The question can be answered in the light of the many critical points which have been made by our own members and by others.

DO THE FUNDS COMPLEMENT THE WAGE SOLIDARITY POLICY?

Some people postulate that any scheme which is intended to reinforce solidarity in wage policy has got to make it possible to redistribute the ability to pay wages between firms and sectors, so they are unlikely to feel particularly satisfied with the solution which the employee investment funds offer. We have set out our reasons for rejecting any idea of such a redistribution. But the problem with wage solidarity is not primarily one of making the 'excess profits' of high-pay companies disposable as potential wage increases for low-paid groups. We can assume that strong unions do exploit the whole of the potential that is available for pay increases. The problem is rather that the policy of solidarity ought not to favour owners of capital in high-profit companies. Possible solutions to the problem are to be found in branch funds, higher corporation tax and employee funds. We recommend the last for reasons which we have argued in detail. Can such employee funds then be said to constitute a support for wage solidarity?

The growth of the funds is linked to profits. To the extent that profits arise in profitable enterprises (more accurately, to the extent that profits are higher than they would have been if profitability had varied with wage setting) because a policy of wage solidarity continues to be pursued in the future, these excess profits will gradually accrue to the whole employee collective. The high-wage groups who demonstrate their solidarity with their low-wage comrades need not fear that the fruits of this cohesion will benefit private owners. Thus the funds can provide strong support, and indeed prove a fundamental condition, for solidarity in pay policy.

It has been argued that the fund capital can only be accumulated in profitable firms, and that employee influence through co-ownership is therefore confined to these companies. A further alleged weakness is that small private companies and the whole of the public sector are not to participate in the build-up of the funds and that in these cases the employees are left right outside the system. This is true; but it is no more than a half-truth. Other factors have to be noticed as well. There are no watertight bulkheads between the 4,000 firms which would be included on our proposal and the 245,000 which would remain outside. The larger firms employ over $1\frac{1}{2}$ million people, the smaller 800,000, and frequently employees do not remain in 'their' particular group of companies for the whole of their working lives. There is considerable mobility between firms, sectors, occupations and regions. Nor is there a clear boundary between the private and public labour markets. In the course of their working lives many employees traverse the boundary several times between companies which are assumed to be in the scheme and others which are excluded. A person working in a small firm who considers that the employee investment fund system does not concern him may prove to be taking too narrow a view. Later in life he may move to a larger firm, or his company may become part of a large concern. His small firm may also be a subcontractor to another company in which employee influence is greater, and that may help to support the subcontractor.

Even more important, however, is the point that the income from the fund will benefit every employee, and that people employed in small firms will enjoy the priorities which we discussed in Chapter 6. An arrangement of this nature is an expression of solidarity, between those groups which have been able to use their trade union strength at their place of employment to increase the influence of employees and other groups of workers for whom the small size of their firm and other factors make it more difficult to pursue an improvement in the working environment and greater democracy. On a long view, this kind of cohesion may well develop into an important support for wage solidarity.

Given these conditions, therefore, the system of employee funds can accordingly be regarded as providing moral and substantive support for the wages policy. We discern in some of the criticisms of this reasoning a hint of a critical attitude towards the wage solidarity policy as such. Those who are eager to see groups who are already highly paid enjoying local bargaining cannot be expected to applaud proposals which are intended to strengthen union solidarity. All we need remark here is that the 1971 and 1976 LO Congresses gave stronger support than ever before to the idea of continuing along the road of solidarity in wage policy.

WILL THE FUNDS REDUCE THE CONCENTRATION OF OWNERSHIP?

As we have observed earlier, the employee investment funds can only counter the concentration of wealth in a quantitatively small part of our national assets: the companies sector. Critics have frequently pointed to this limitation, and asked why the redistribution of property should be limited to shareholders in particular, while accepting the much greater inequities that exist in more important sectors, such as the real estate market.

There are two answers to this criticism. The first is that the trade union movement does not accept the present distribution of ownership in any sector, particularly the shocking injustices which have occurred and are continually occurring through speculation in land. These injustices should be rectified by tax policy, but that is not an adequate reason for refraining from employee funds, which have other and broader objectives. Secondly, share ownership as a form of ownership differs widely from other categories of ownership. This is so self-evident that it really ought not to require further comment. But a lot of people have claimed, probably out of hypocrisy rather than ignorance, that they fail to see in what ways the ownership of shares is unique, so we take the following example to illustrate this obvious truth.

About 600,000 Swedes own second homes. If we value each of these properties at 75,000 crowns, second homes represent a capital asset worth about 45,000 million crowns. A small proportion of this is borrowed capital, but the net property is probably worth about the same as the shares of quoted companies. It is not unlikely that inflation and the rise in land prices provide the owners of second homes with an annual profit on their property which is no less than that of shareholders. It can be argued that the inequities that exist between the 700,000 Swedes who do own shares and all the rest who do not are no greater than those between the 600,000 owners of second homes and the large majority who do not possess one.

The point of the example is not to lend support to this view but to demonstrate its weakness. The owner of a leisure home has made an investment, the yield from which he consumes in the form of accommodation services for recreational purposes. He makes no decisions and takes no actions which determine the employment and livelihood of other people. The shareholder, on the other hand, owns part of the apparatus of production which is used in a production process during which additional capital is formed. Directly or indirectly, the shareholder has a right of decision over the way in which production resources are to be deployed, augmented, removed, merged or scrapped. It is this right of decision, which brings consequences for the employment of other people, for the continued existence of the community and for the whole national economy, which gives the ownership of shares a unique status as a strategic form of ownership, and that is why it is important to check any continued concentration of private ownership.

But does the establishment of a number of employee funds really signify that this process of concentration will cease or even be curtailed? We mentioned earlier that the stock market is in the process of becoming more 'institutionalised', in the sense that the proportion of private shareholders is declining in favour of institutional investors such as insurance companies, the fourth National Pension Fund, investment companies, foundations and unit trusts. True, new groups of savers are holding shares, but previous share-owning groups are turning to new investment objects. It may be thought that the establishment of employee funds will reinforce this process of institutionalisation, that it will hasten concentration in the hands of major stockholders. People who are reluctant to discern any significant difference between shares and second leisure homes as forms of ownership will certainly not detect any difference between the institutional holdings which currently dominate the market and the employee investment funds. It will simply mean that one power group replaces another. The most vulgar formulations of this assertion argue that private ownership will be superseded by autocratic and bureaucratic funds.

With a few exceptions, such as some insurance companies and the National Pension Fund, the institutions which manage portfolios of shares are not organised in a democratic fashion. They represent remnants of a society in which ownership is carried forward and strengthened from generation to generation through inheritance, successful entrepreneurship and family loyalty. The employee funds will be democratically administered institutions devoid of private profit and power aspiration. The managers of the central fund will not be able to act as bigwigs, since the fund will only administer assets which cannot be realised and possess certain powers in allocating income for a variety of purposes. In glaring contrast to the real economic power centres of the day, the central fund, which has been such a key target in the propaganda against the funds idea, is a body which has no power other than that of administering resources and income. It is a supreme authority which has nothing and no one to command, a bureaucracy without bureaucrats, and a power centre which has no power.

The real 'power' rests with the board members in the individual companies who will for the duration of a lengthy build-up period be appointed by the employees themselves, and thereafter by democratically elected fund boards on the nomination of the employees. In that sense the employee funds will mean that it becomes more difficult to have a concentration of share ownership and that the employees – not the central trade union bodies – will acquire the right to dispose over a larger proportion of the shareholdings. Out of either ignorance or malevolence it has been suggested that on our construction employee funds will increase the power of the trade union organisations at the expense of the individual worker. In fact the system involves the extensive decentralisation of influence. The shareholding will be registered centrally, but the rights to which it gives an entitlement will accrue to the body of employees in the workplace. This no threat to, but a pre-requisite for, real influence. The term 'owner democracy' has been abused as a cloak for a number of sham solutions and can therefore not be used here. But what we can say is that employee funds are a method of democratising ownership.

WILL EMPLOYEE FUNDS RESULT IN MORE EMPLOYEE INFLUENCE?

'Power' and 'Influence' are concepts which people who exercise power of various kinds are reluctant to use. Talk of more employee power therefore strikes many people as shocking. What the 1971 LO Congress was searching for, however, was a system which makes it possible to increase the influence which employees can exercise on the basis of capital contributed. We have just been arguing that employee funds reduce the growth of capital on the part of private owners, and that this therefore reduces their power as well. But does it follow from this that employee influence will expand, that the funds will become an instrument for making work more democratic? Critics have asserted that the fund system gives the individual employee neither real ownership nor influence. The funds have been projected as a tool of trade union power aspirations and an authoritarian mentality.

Union influence can be brought to bear on two different planes: first in relation to conditions at the place of work; and second with regard to more all-embracing questions, for example of an industrial policy nature. We have explained in detail in the preceding chapters how the employee funds can strengthen and extend union influence on both planes. The most immediate thing is the support for union influence at the local level, and this is the main object of the major reforms in labour legislation. Here the income of the fund is intended to strengthen union resources. In this connection tens of thousands of union members should be able to derive specific and obvious benefit from the improvements in training, information flows and other possible activities.

In due course, as the resources of the fund increase, the second range of union influence will gather momentum; there will be growing possibilities for the unions to influence the more comprehensive and strategic decisions which management makes. Employee representatives will participate increasingly in these decisions. They will be appointed by their workmates, but they will have access to specialist assistance from, and consultation with, the sector funds or regional councils, thereby obtaining a better basis for their assessments than would be the case if they had to rely on data emanating from the firm. When critics express the view that this arrangement for the funds does not augment the influence which is available to the individual employee they are simply expressing their distrust of representative democracy and in reality defending the existing disposition of power within industry.

WILL EMPLOYEE FUNDS AFFECT INVESTMENT AND EMPLOYMENT?

Two completely incompatible points of view have been put forward in the controversy about employee funds. According to the first, the system of funds can and should be made an instrument for increasing investment; capital formation is regarded as a quite critical aim of economic policy. On the other view, the system of funds and the construction proposed for it will hamper investment and thus endanger employment. In our introductory chapter we declared our intention of designing the system in such a way that the system itself did not alter the relationship between consumption and saving. Nor, however, should the solution adopted impede the amount of capital formation which the authorities regard as desirable. To put it another way, the fund system should be neutral from the point of view of capital formation.

We can note right away that we need a high volume of saving in Sweden if we are to satisfy the important investment needs which are essential to her balance of payments, to the desired improvement in the standard of living, and for increasing the aid which she gives to underdeveloped countries. In 1974 the gross saving ratio reached its lowest level since the mid-1950s, at just over 20 per cent of the national product. The decline could be attributed entirely to the large reduction in public saving, including the National Pension Fund, while the household saving share actually increased. The fact that investment did not decline in step with the fall in saving was entirely due to large-scale borrowing abroad by Sweden. The Long-Term Survey argues that the most important task facing economic policy in the period to 1980 is that of increasing domestic saving sufficiently to finance Sweden's investment requirements out of her own resources while at the same time reducing her indebtedness. The indications are that this objective cannot be attained until the 1980s.

From our point of view, the trend in industrial investment is of particular interest. The Long-Term Survey considered that the required growth of exports and also the continued growth of public expenditure would necessitate a strong increase in industrial investment. It estimated that private investment in industry would, in the late 1970s, have to increase its share considerably above the level that has prevailed at any time since 1950. The methods of financing these additional investments in industry raise a very important question of distribution policy. The degree of industrial self-financing declined substantially between the 1950s and 1960s, but increased again during the favourable years 1973 and 1974. There has been a clear tendency to rely more heavily on external sources of capital. Another method of expressing this is to say that the solvency level of business firms, i.e. the proportion of total capital constituted by equity capital, has fallen heavily since about 1960.

The government will probably endorse these assessments by the Long-Term Planning Commission, which means that efforts will be made via various policy measures to stimulate investment in industry. The alternative recommended in business quarters is that of relying mainly on higher profitability and increased self-financing, though it is frankly recognised that high profit retentions as savings involve 'a rapid rise in shareholders' wealth, a sharp departure from the aim of equalising the distribution of wealth'.[1]

A more correct approach from the standpoint of distribution would be to increase public saving. We noted a moment ago that it was the reductions in public saving which were mainly responsible for the decline in the total saving ratio. The most convenient solution would be to increase employer contributions as a means of restoring the previous relationship between public and private saving.

By contrast, the employee funds have very long-term duties to discharge, and they ought not to be used as a vehicle for increasing capital formation. At present and for perhaps the next five years more investment will be important, but it is inappropriate to get this mixed up with the main aim of the fund system, that of bringing about a long-term shift in the structure of ownership for the benefit of employees. The system can on the other hand play an important part in facilitating the capital formation which the community sets for itself and can achieve by other means. Even if these consist principally of an increase in public saving, the levels of self-financing of the 1960s will mean that most of the capital comes from company profits. It is obvious that a situation of this nature would be easier to accept on distributive grounds if part of the increase in assets generated via self-financing were to accrue to employees as a group than if, as in the past, this simply brought

[1] Olle Lindgren and Erik Lundberg, 'Overcoming the shortage of saving', in *Skandinaviska Enskilda Banken Quarterly Review*, No. 3, 1975, p. 107.

about a further increase in the assets of the former share-holders. In that sense, but only in that sense, can the employee fund system be said to favour more capital formation.

Exactly the opposite argument has been advanced from another quarter; not only can the employee funds not contribute to an increase in capital formation, they risk enfeebling investment by frightening risk capital away and undermining companies' willingness to invest.

There is no denying that every authentic sharing of profits must mean that some part of the future profit is transferred from the original owners to the employees. The stock market operates in such a way as to discount these reduced profit expectations, and in all probability results in a fall in share prices for the previous owners. Once this discounting has occurred, share prices ought to stabilise again and the yield be related to the lower prices. For future purchasers of shares the situation regarding profitability is not much altered, on the assumption that the market fully discounts the anticipated effects of the system of funds.

The fund system does not differ in these respects from other profit-sharing systems which do not only appear to, but really do, give the employees a share in the profits. Those systems which involve saving part of the wage, e.g. investment wage systems, or which mean that the employees receive profit shares instead of a wage, are of course not a burden on the share-holders and do not have the effects which we have just discussed. They ought in all honesty to be called compulsory saving, wage saving or bonus wages, but not profit sharing.

These fears of adverse effects on capital formation apply not only to employee funds but to every proper profit-sharing system; but this does not make the criticism any the less relevant. This is of course somewhat curious, since it is sometimes made by the same people who themselves recommend such profit-sharing systems.

No one can predict with certainty how the stock market would react to the introduction of an employee investment fund system. Even very knowledgeable judges are rather uncertain. No experience can be cited. As far as we are aware, the profit-sharing system which the Swedish Handelsbank operates, for instance, has not led to a flight of shareholders, although they are having to help to finance a fund owned by the employees. But it is not improbable that stock market quotations will fall as a consequence of the appropriation of profit which we propose. This type of appropriation has been likened to a tax, and it has been argued that it will have the same effects. Let us assume that it is technically and legally feasible. How is it likely to affect the supply of new risk capital?

We have already remarked that our stock market is in the process of changing its structure towards an ever-growing proportion of institutional shareholders, with a corresponding decline in private individuals as shareholders. It may be that keen propaganda as to the allegedly harmful effects of the funds will frighten away some private individuals, at least for a time. Increasingly dominant operators, including the fourth National Pension Fund, will only refrain from share purchases, however, if they find other investments more attractive. It is difficult to believe, particularly in an economy in which the value of money is steadily declining, that the establishment of employee funds would make the stock market lose its attractiveness for this latter group of investors. The strong rise in the stock market in recent years, when profitability has been greatly reduced, demonstrates that the stock market is remarkably resilient to bigger strains in the matter of yield than any that a system of employee funds could cause.

We conclude that the fears of a decline in the supply of risk capital are considerably exaggerated. It should also be remembered that the increment of risk capital from shareholders plays an extremely small part in the financing of investment. In the period 1966 to 1970, self-financing, i.e. companies' own saving, accounted for approximately half the finance, banks and the capital market for 10 per cent, and short-term borrowing for no less than 38 per cent (an abnormally high figure which must have been due to the exceptional conditions in 1970). Share issues, the risk capital in the proper sense of the term, amounted to only 3 per cent of the total. However important access to this form of capital may be, it thus plays an extremely insignificant part in the finance of industrial investment. The possibilities of other external sources of finance and self-financing are the decisive factors.

Even if the supply of risk capital will probably not decline significantly as a consequence of the introduction of employee funds, it may be that companies will show less appetite for investment. Not surprisingly, the debate about employee funds has thrown up a number of reasons in support of this thesis. The prospect of the former owners having in future to share their profits for the benefit of employees would make management reluctant to invest in growth, it is argued. Investment abroad would appear more attractive. The already weak position of family firms would be worsened. There would be little excitement in launching new enterprises. And so on.

These arrangements are scarcely founded on fact. The total profitability of companies is not altered through the introduction of a system of funds. Their solidity is strengthened. Increased influence for employees is likely to support the growth of companies rather than the reverse. But these arguments from the side of business are the expression of a negative reaction to the thought that the structure of ownership and power in industry is going to change. It would be foolish not to consider this reaction and its consequences for the private propensity to invest as a factor to be reckoned with, and to seek to counter it. If, for instance, the system of funds were to be introduced in an atmosphere of strong political disagreement, the reaction could be a painful economic fact, particularly during the critical early years of building up the funds. Some of the participants in the LO study campaign doubted whether, in fact, such a situation could be overcome.

The government obviously cannot leave investment and

therefore employment to its own fate, in this or in any other situation. We discussed in an earlier chapter the question of multinational firms, which disturbs many of LO's members. We can assume that the community's knowledge of and control over these enterprises will have been considerably improved by the time the introduction of employee funds becomes imminent. Government industrial policy is being steadily strengthened and can be activated in the event of a drop in the private willingness to invest. Tax policy provides a further instrument for influencing the willingness to invest in a positive way. If the decision to introduce employee funds is made in the normal democratic manner, this very fact gives the government a mandate to use appropriate policy measures to ensure that the reform does not lead to an investment strike, reduced capital formation and a drop in employment. There would undoubtedly be very strong popular support for the idea of taking the necessary countermeasures, should such a situation arise.

ARE THE FUNDS NEUTRAL WITH RESPECT TO COSTS, PRICES AND PAY?

Every known profit-sharing system involves funds being removed from the enterprise and transferred, with or without an interval of time, to the employees. The enterprise must regard this as a cost item, equivalent to a wage increase. The increase in cost justifies higher prices. Whether this can be done depends on many factors, including the construction of the system. If the profit shares are available for consumption, this increases total purchasing power. If the funds are tied for a period, e.g. through some arrangement for saving or in the form of share purchases, enterprises may find it more difficult to implement price increases. However they are constructed, these systems are clearly not neutral as regards costs and prices, and this makes it impossible to assess whether the employees as a group do or do not obtain a higher share of company saving.

An employee investment fund system, in which the funds never leave the firm, is, by contrast, neutral with respect to costs. Nor have the critics argued in the debate about the funds that they would raise costs and prices. What they have suggested, however, is the possibility that firms would raise prices in order to compensate their shareholders for the reduction in yield in consequence of the profit sharing. If the gradual transfer of company profits to the employees is regarded as a tax on net profits, it is impossible to argue at the same time that this tax could be shifted on to the consumers. There is in any case no purchasing power available to meet this shifting, in the event of no profit shares being disbursed in cash to the employees.

Nor is any attempt on the part of companies to shift this 'taxation' backwards, i.e. to compensate the former shareholders through an equivalent reduction in wages (though it would be more realistic to think of a lower rate of increase in wages), likely to succeed. Swedish wage policy follows what is termed the EFO model; that it to say, it is determined in the main by productivity increases in the export industries and the course of international prices.[1] In a certain sense this can be regarded as the scope or potential which is available for increases in pay, and this is not altered as a result of a redistribution of ownership between owners of capital and employees. In principle, therefore, the employee investment funds are also neutral with respect to wage policy.

[1] See G. Edgren, K-O. Faxén and C-E. Odhner, *Wage Formation and the Economy*, London, 1973, for an analysis along these lines.

Chapter 9

Conclusion

Only a very small minority, just over 5 per cent, of those who took part in the LO study campaign on the subject have rejected the concept of employee funds as a means of reinforcing the influence of the trade unions. Of course one cannot conclude from this that the vast majority of the membership of LO are positive in their attitude to the proposal. The only safe conclusion we can draw is that people whose attitude was already unfavourable have not participated to any extent in the study campaign which LO mounted.

What is more interesting than this rather trite conclusion is the make-up of this group which rejected the idea. It consists mainly of three categories: the largest considers that the proposal is not socialistic enough, the second rejects it as being far too socialistic, while the third considers that the funds will lead to the wrong kind of socialism. Despite the modest size of this negatively disposed group, these differences within it do provide some indication of the difficulty we face in attaching some kind of ideological label to a society in which there is a growth of employee funds. Are we speaking still of a mixed economy? Is it a stage on the road to a socialist society? Does it lead to a concentration of power in the hands of a few trade union organisations who simultaneously lose the capacity to safeguard their members' interests? Would it mean that we were on the way to a corporate form of society?

We have sketched in as detailed a form as possible a system of funds which can be considered to meet the requirements specified in our assignment. To ask what ideological label is to be attached to a society with employee funds is to us a secondary question. None the less, the question has featured in the debate, so it is worth making a few observations on it by way of conclusion.

There are no clear and generally accepted definitions as to what is meant by the 'mixed economy'. The mixture can refer to various considerations, such as varieties of ownership, and the element of planning in an economy based on the principles of the market economy. As regards ownership the Swedish economy is scarcely a mixed one at all; much more than most West European economies, it is dominated by private ownership, and there has been no appreciable change in this situation for many years. In respect of planning there has on the other hand been a sustained movement towards greater social influence over the economy.

If anything does typify the Swedish economy it is surely the mixture of an extremely modest degree of social ownership and a soaring ambition with regard to social influence over the course of economic events. This combination of private ownership and social control over the economy can in fact be said to constitute the foundation of the Swedish variation on the theme of the mixed economy.

The introduction of employee funds would mean the emergence of a new category of owner which would gain ground at the expense of private ownership. The structure of ownership in the mixed Swedish economy would then be altered, but the framework of the mixed economy would not be shattered; private ownership would continue to dominate, while other forms of ownership, through socially owned and consumer co-operative enterprises, would not be affected. But in a regime with employee funds, can a mixed economy be preserved in the long run, in the sense that wages are determined through bargaining between free negotiating parties, and the community is strong enough to conduct a policy *vis-à-vis* the trade unions (who would become both negotiating party and capital owner) which is determined solely by the will of the people? Would our society remain 'open' and 'pluralistic', to use highly respected terms which nevertheless do express fundamental values in our contemporary society?

There are no inherent forces at work in a correctly articulated system of employee funds which inexorably erode these values. They are values not because they are part of a mixed economy, but because they constitute parts of our democracy. The unions will still be able to represent employee interests as well where there is a growing element of employee ownership in the form of collectively owned employee funds. However much this ownership may increase in the future, the unions will also have to bow to political decisions.

The question is not one of an insoluble conflict of roles but of the need to find the appropriate organisational forms for allocating roles. The trade union movement as a pressure group, the employee funds as a form of ownership, and society as the instrument of the political will of the people have sometimes been presented as mutually incompatible phenomena. There is greater justification for the argument that the establishment of employee funds could support both the trade union struggle on behalf of their members' interests and the political battle on behalf of the interests of the citizens. The collective employee fund model gradually eliminates the residue of a society of class and privilege in our otherwise democratic welfare society. One does not recede further from the 'open society' by giving employees more influence over economic affairs than they enjoy at present. Democracy is not put at risk by extending the basis of economic decision making. The unions are not enervated by making employees as a group into owners of capital; what one does is to alter and expand their responsibilities. It is not a question, as non-socialist critics have alleged, of threatening the mixed economy, but of using the employee funds to preserve it against the threats of the massive concentration of economic power in a handful of large industrial companies with an increasingly unequal ownership structure.

By virtue of its character, aims and likely effects the proposal to establish employee funds is a reformist one, involving as it does one element in a step-by-step policy, where no step is taken into the unknown but each step is taken only when the ground underneath appears firm. This approach on the part of the Swedish democratic labour movement has always provoked two sets of opponents: one which considers that Swedish society must be changed root and branch in one single decisive stride and the other which is opposed to change and seeks to safeguard the status quo. It is a familiar pattern that a reformist proposal such as that for employee funds is distrusted by the social revolutionaries as a defence of the old class order and by the conservatives as a social revolution. Both these groups have demonstrated that they are persistent losers when it comes to having some influence on the way society develops. Employee funds are not intended as a deviation from, but as a new step on the long road towards, our continuing goal of equality and economic democracy.

Appendix I

LO Members Assess the Funds-the Consultative Process

As we indicated in the Preface, and as has become clear from the discussion in the text, the views of some 18,000 (1 per cent) of the members of LO unions about the proposed funds were elicited in the autumn of 1975. Study groups were formed which discussed material prepared by the authors of this study on the basis of their first draft report. Certain questions were also posed, and the replies were analysed. No attempt is made to reproduce here the whole survey and the categories of answers, since these are referred to in summary in the discussion in the main text. It may be helpful, however, to indicate the nature and range of questions and answers.

Employee Investment Funds

Questions	Responses (%)	
1 How important is ownership for employee influence?	Absolutely necessary	69·1
	Important	20·6
	Some significance	8·1
	Of no importance	0·8
	Disadvantageous	1·4
		100·0
2 Ought individual profit-sharing systems to be introduced?	Yes	8·4
	No	91·6
		100·0
3 For what purposes ought the yield from the funds to be used? (Suggested uses were indicated in the study material, but participants could add their own suggestions.)	Collective purposes	94·6
	Cash distributions	4·9
	Combination of these	0·5
		100·0
4 What type of fund should administer the income? (Other questions were asked under this heading about election of board members, representation of the public interest.)	Central	50·5
	Branch	5·1
	Regional	10·1
	Company	6·1
	Central + branch	4·3
	Central + regional	15·7
	Other	8·2
		100·0
5 What is your view of excess profits?	No problem even at present	2·6
	Of less interest if employee funds introduced	39·6
	Ought to be tapped even if funds introduced	57·8
		100·0
6 Participants' own comments, e.g. on spread of system by size of firm – an open-ended question		

Appendix II

Recent Reforms in Swedish Labour Legislation

A number of important enactments in recent years have helped to promote industrial democracy and employees' rights.

The *Security of Employment Act* 1974 provides protection against unfair dismissal and requires an employer to show cause for dismissing employees. Minimum periods of notice of termination of employment are also specified. In the same year the *Promotion of Employment Act* was passed, and it requires employers to notify the public labour market authorities of planned cut-backs in manpower and to enter into discussions about the proposals. The Act also introduced arrangements for improving job prospects for older and handicapped people through the setting-up of adjustment teams in workplaces.

The status of shop stewards was also strengthened in 1974 by a legal enactment, and this was significant in giving the unions preferential rights with regard to the interpretation of the Act in the event of disputes between an employer and unions about its application. The *Workers' Protection Act* was also amended in 1974, to reflect the widening interests in the social and psychological as well as the physical aspects of hazards on the job. Legislation on paid educational leave was passed in 1975, and this gives the unions substantial rights in the interpretation of the Act and over the appropriate education and training activities which may be arranged.

Much of the influence and insight which employees have been able to acquire in the past over the running of the enterprises for which they work has been structured around joint consultative committees, or works councils, which have been set up in many companies as a result of a central agreement between LO and SAF dating from 1946. Over the years these bodies have improved the flow of information on a consultative basis, but a big step was taken from consultation to co-determination in 1972, when experimental legislation was passed providing for representation on company boards of employees of companies. Under the legislation companies with a hundred employees or more could be required by trade unions which were parties to collective agreements with them and which represented over half the workforce to have two board members appointed from among the employees, if the staff decided that they did wish to have this form of representation. Employee board members were not permitted to take part in business which concerned industrial relations and collective bargaining. The experiment developed satisfactorily, and in 1976 the legislation was put on a more permanent basis, with the threshold for the number of employees being reduced from a hundred to twenty-five.

Joint consultation and representation on boards have certainly increased the formal and actual flow of information. Often, however, this information, for example about company finances, is complex and technical. As a means of providing a 'back-up' service for employee directors and other employee representatives in companies, an agreement was negotiated between LO and SAF in 1975 which provides for the establishment of economic committees or the appointment of employee consultants. This agreement provides (in order of preference) three alternatives – an internal economic committee, internal consultants or externally appointed consultants, whose task it is to ensure that employees are provided with expert reports about the economic affairs of companies. Those appointed to committees or as consultants are therefore expected to have expertise in accounting and business economics. The employer meets all costs involved.

All these enactments and arrangements reflect the growing momentum of employee pressure for greater economic democracy and involvement in industrial decision making. The keystone of this process is the *Act on the Joint Regulation of Working Life*. This Act is based on the work of a Royal Commission appointed in 1971, and it came into force at the beginning of 1977. The Act substantially erodes the traditional prerogatives of management and gives unions the right to call for co-determination agreements. The Act carries forward the existing arrangements under legislation covering Collective Agreements (1928), the Right of Association and Collective Bargaining (1936) and the Mediation Act (1920), and envisages that collective agreements will continue to be the main vehicle for regulating relationships between employees and their employers. The following are the main themes covered by the Act.

The area of negotiation between the parties to agreements is substantially broadened to cover important changes in the employer's business, such as the reorganisation of production, organisational changes and transfer of ownership. The employer has *a primary duty to negotiate* on these matters, in the sense that he must take the initiative in promoting negotiations with the unions concerned. In principle, he cannot initiate and implement changes until he has done this.

The employer is now required to provide *a regular flow of information* to unions with which he has agreements on the economics, production and personnel policies of his firm. Unions are also entitled to ask for additional information via access to books, accounts and other documents. Disputes about confidentiality of information can be referred in the last resort to the national Labour Court for a ruling.

The core of the *Act* is the concept of *negotiated joint influence or participation agreements*. Parties are expected to enter into such agreements covering contracts of employment, direction and allocation of work, and the conduct of the business with regard to manpower and personnel matters. The deliberate intention here is to move away from the old management concept of the right to hire and fire. A union can put pressure on an employer to conclude such an agreement by virtue of its having *a residual right of industrial action* if the employer refuses to enter into such an agreement. The union can only demand that such an agreement be concluded in the context of wage bargaining; but if the employer refuses the union can resort to industrial action even if it is otherwise bound by a collective agreement. This is a major departure from the traditional rule that all industrial action was banned for the duration of a collective agreement. A union can only call for such residual action in accordance with its rules, which usually reserve to the national executive the right to call stoppages of work.

The Act also gives unions *priority of interpretation* in certain matters, first with regard to the interpretation of a joint influence agreement, and secondly in disputes about an employee's duties and work obligations. This reverses the traditional right of the employer to have the initiative. Under the new arrangement disputes can still proceed as 'rights disputes' to the Labour Court. In a third area of rights disputes, that of disputed wage issues, the employer's right to decide is substantially abridged; his interpretation has priority for a period of ten days, after which the union view will prevail unless the employer has in the meantime asked for the difference to be referred to national level.

When this Act was passed the government envisaged that a major education drive would be needed to ensure that these fundamental changes were understood. LO has also launched a major campaign to ensure that its affiliates understand their entitlements. The role of the proposed employee investment funds and their income is clearly relevant to this process. Whole new areas of collective bargaining potential are being opened up, and the trade union movement must insist that it has the resources to train its people to deal with them.

Index